Employability: From Theory to Practice

International Social Security Series

In cooperation with the
International Social Security Association (ISSA)
Neil Gilbert, Series Editor

Employability: From Theory to Practice

editors
Patricia Weinert, Michèle Baukens,
Patrick Bollérot, Marina Pineschi-Gapènne,
and Ulrich Walwei

International Social Security Series
Volume 7

Transaction Publishers
New Brunswick (U.S.A.) and London (U.K.)

The International Social Security Association (ISSA) was founded in 1927. It is a nonprofit international organization bringing together institutions and administrative bodies from countries all over the world dealing with all forms of compulsory social protection. The objective of the ISSA is to cooperate at the international level, in the promotion and development of social security throughout the world, primarily by improving techniques and administration in order to advance people's social and economic conditions on the basis of social justice.

This book is printed on acid-free paper that meets the American National Standard for Permanence of Paper for Printed Library Materials.

Library of Congress Number: 2001027201
ISBN: 0-7658-0879-X
Printed in the United States of America

Library of Congress Cataloging-in-Publication Data

Employablility: from theory to practice / Patricia Weinert ... [et a.], editors.
      p. cm. — (International social security series; v. 7)
   Includes bibliographical references and index.
   ISBN 0-7658-0879-X (pbk.: alk. paper)
     1. Manpower policy—Case studies. I. Weinert, Patricia. II. Series.

HD5713 .E467 2001
331.11—dc21   2001027201

Contents

New Zealand
Poland and Slovakia
Algeria

Part 3: Trends

Preface

Employability is a complex notion and the subject of many debates. The European Commission has made employability one of the priority thrusts of its strategy on employment, and numerous unemployment systems have integrated the promotion of employability into their mechanisms.

In order to make its contribution to this debate, which is both current and permanently evolving, the Technical Commission on Unemployment Insurance and Employment Maintenance of the International Social Security Association (ISSA) decided in 1998 to undertake the publication of a work taking into account both the theoretical and practical aspects of this set of problems.

Different authors, stemming primarily from unemployment insurance institutions and scientific milieux, were requested to deal with a precise theme or a national experience.

A working group composed of Patricia Weinert (ISSA), Marina Pineschi-Gapenne and Patrick Bollérot, *Union nationale interprofessionnelle pour l'emploi dans l'industrie et le commerce* (UNEDIC), France, Michèle Baukens, *Office national de l'emploi* (ONEM) and Ulrich Walwei, *Bundesanstalt für Arbeit* (BA), Germany, was entrusted with coordinating and analyzing the various contributions and drawing trends and views therefrom.

At each of its stages, the accomplishment of this work was followed attentively and overseen by the members of the Bureau of the Technical Commission.

On behalf of all the members of the Commission, we wish to thank sincerely all those who have participated in the preparation of this publication. In so doing, they have contributed to the enrichment of the debate on employability. However, it should be noted here that the views expressed in this publication are those of the authors and not necessarily those of the Technical Commission nor of the ISSA.

We hope that this volume will constitute a valuable working tool and a fruitful source of inspiration for both decision-makers and researchers.

Karel Baeck (ONEM)
Jean-Pierre Revoil (UNEDIC)
Otto Semmler (BA)
Members of the Bureau of the Technical Commission on
Unemployment Insurance and Employment Maintenance (ISSA)

Introduction

In the struggle against unemployment and marginalization, employability has developed into one major tool to counteract this phenomenon. While the notion of employability is not exactly new, the weight now being placed upon it is new: to equip job-seekers for the changes currently taking place in the economy and the world of work.

The increasing pace of globalization and technological change no doubt provides challenges for economic expansion and job creation but at the same time increases job insecurity and job displacement, as well as a growing risk of exclusion from employment for the unskilled. Hence, the most fundamental challenge for many countries is to increase employment and to combat high unemployment rates using a preventive approach by way of improving a job-seeker's employability rather than merely resorting to curative means.

However, for the purpose of *employability promotion* some essential trends in the world of work need to be borne in mind so as to develop suitable policy measures.

New information technologies are opening the way for automation and greater flexibility, having important repercussions on the division of labor in enterprises, on decentralization, on the association of information systems (multimedia) as well as on the temporal and spatial separation of the worker from the machine. There is a revival of home work and self-employment.

The chances of long-term prosperity for the provision of goods and services in a context of international competition vary directly in accordance with their intelligence content, their level of quality or their degree of specialization (high technology, high degree of specialization, grouped services, systemic solutions, etc.) and the extent to which new markets are explored and opened up. *Knowledge* is becoming the essential resource.

Structural change fosters the creation of small and medium-sized organizational units and increases the number of worker-entrepreneurs. The "normal employment relationship" of the industrial age, with its rigidities and status of dependency, is becoming more and more relaxed. This process is promoting the emergence of new forms of employment, also referred to as "atypical." Part-time jobs, temporary and casual employment, employment on detachment and teleworking have thus brought a new heterogeneity to the world of work.

All these changes open up new areas of skilled service activities such as research and development, organization and management, consultancy, publication and teaching, as well as the installation and maintenance of machinery. The segment of the services sector which is likely to expand most is the information-linked segment. Evidence shows that we are progressing towards a society of services and information.

As a result, the level and quality of skills required are rising and becoming critical factors. Technical competencies and expertise in methods and social questions are also called for. What is more, demand will be increasingly directed towards essential competencies such as flexibility, initiative and creativity; a basic knowledge of several occupations and a good general education; the will and ability to take action independently and with full responsibility and to continually seek improvement and cooperate with others.

Finally, in view of the ageing of the active population resulting from the arrival of the smaller age groups, structural change will increasingly have to be conducted by middle-aged and older active persons instead of by generation replacement.

In the face of these far-reaching changes in the world of work, it is argued that those who have no chances to develop or enhance their employability will fail in the competitive labor market in the new economic order.

In order to respond adequately to these challenges, the European Employment Strategy has declared employability to be one of its four priority areas of action. Although not often defined, employability, in the sense of the European Commission's definition, aims at dynamic and updated competencies and labor-market-oriented behavior for every person participating in the workforce. Employability should improve the employment situation, as well as equip the workforce to adapt to the demands of the twenty-first century labor markets.

Accordingly, the guaranteeing and the improvement of employability constitute a complex undertaking, because it is not a static concept. It is rather referred to as a broad policy agenda.

The questions which therefore arise are manifold: Is employability a response to maintain the balance between increasing flexibility and decreasing security? Is employability in the future the defining policy framework for labor market policies? Does the notion of employability imply that the responsibility to be (more) employable lies solely on the individual's initiative? And, if income maintenance programs do not anymore provide adequate security, will (reactive) unemployment insurance schemes turn into (proactive) employability insurances? What are the consequences of such a development for policy-makers?

The articles presented in this volume seek to provide a contribution to the conceptual and operational content of the employability notion by addressing some pertinent issues related to the above questions. This publication attempts to clarify complex policy questions which hopefully will contribute to a better understanding of the concept. By doing so, it is equally intended to provide an insight into both the *possibilities* and *limitations* of employability promotion measures, since *employability* is not a panacea to solve all problems encountered in today's labor markets. It has its limits to what can be achieved in terms of fighting unemployment. Furthermore, employability should certainly not be a substitute for other policy measures necessary to improve labor market conditions.

This introduction provides a brief description of the contents of this publication. The material is basically presented in three parts:

- Part 1 deals with concepts and instruments of employability and contains four chapters. Chapter 1 introduces the complexity of the employability notion. It is followed by chapter 2, which focuses on one particular technique used for early identification of potential long-term unemployed. The role of the employer and the worker in the employability process is analyzed in chapter 3, whilst chapter 4 addresses the question of whether European unemployment insurance schemes are turning towards an employability insurance model.

- Part 2 contains country papers describing and, to the extent possible, evaluating measures implemented, with the objective of improving employability of job-seekers. The dimension of the labor market is well reflected when analyzing the problem of unemployment traps and their impact on an individual's effort to reintegrate into the labor force.[1] The countries under review in this volume comprise four members of the European Union (the United Kingdom, the Netherlands, Belgium, Ireland) and one OECD country (New Zealand). It was found particularly relevant to consider the way two countries in transition, Poland and Slovakia, cope with their labor market problems. Furthermore, the unemployment problem confronted by a developing country such as Algeria, which quite recently (1994) introduced an unemployment insurance scheme, and the way in which it is tackling this problem by means of activation measures merits attention.

- In Part 3, a practical approach is being showcased with Canada, which in 1996-97 moved from an unemployment to an employment insurance. The last chapter then briefly reviews the information provided by all contributors and provides an outlook for the future.

Lastly, it should be stressed that by the time this volume is published hopefully new evaluation data might be available since much more research into the effectiveness of employability promotion measures needs to be carried out.

Patricia Weinert
Programme Manager
International Social Security Association (ISSA)

Note

For other labor market related issues dealt with by the Technical Commission, also refer to Spitznagel, "Combating unemployment by means of employment-creation programmes and the development of a secondary labour market," in *Harmonizing Economic Developments and Social Needs,* ISSA, 1998.

Part 1

Concepts and Instruments

1

Employability—The Complexity of a Policy Notion

Bernard Gazier

Introduction

Based on a recent collective study,[1] this contribution will concentrate on the scope and the limits of employability as tools to combat unemployment.

Focusing on employability is an attempt to influence the "supply" side of the labor market, i.e., the workers and their productive capacities and performance, while the "demand" side is made up of the companies' requirements, all of which depend on the growth dynamic. It is evident at once how incomplete and how current this position may be: incomplete, because offers only exist when confronted with a demand; and current, because one rarely encounters an economic policy that seeks to stimulate directly a strong demand for work, in the Keynesian tradition of spurring activity. In the last two decades, most governments have rather relied on a progressive improvement of the supply (of products or work) to re-establish conditions required for growth. Without discussing here the wisdom of this approach, one can conclude that priority has been given to the supply of labor rather than to the demand for it, whether with reference to the qualifications or the availability of the workers or to their salary demands.

In this manner, employability appears as an agenda for "activating" employment expenditures by promoting training programs, placement services, more or less targeted subsidies that favor hiring or maintenance in the job, as well as through a varied gamut of

3

incentives or authoritarian measures aimed at "putting the unemployed back to work." The process is meant to be individualized and preventive, as mirrored in the slogan about trying to shift from "job protection" to "security through employability." The application of such measures varies over time and according to the country and the national traditions as well. It is a changing agenda more than a set of stabilized and precise measures that could be inventoried and assessed as to their effects: an orientation, a tendency of labor market policies.

The variety of these practices goes hand in hand with the plurality of possible definitions of employability. In fact, the idea has existed for a century: the first uses of the term date from the beginning of the twentieth century, and they have provoked many applications and debates, the majority of which emphasize the key role played by the worker's initiatives and abilities.

Some versions of the definition of employability place the responsibility for their own employability squarely on the workers themselves, thereby giving the individual the task of adapting to changes in the labor market. Other versions, such as the *European Employment Strategy* of 1998, have a more balanced content that involves both the social partners and the governments.

Some important questions can be detected behind these experiences and debates: up to what point is it possible or desirable to make the unemployed responsible, if not for their situation, at least for the steps to be taken in order to find a new job? What are the advantages and the dangers in insisting on the concept of employability and in developing policies along those lines?

This study will be divided into three parts. A first historical-conceptual section will briefly review the different operational definitions of employability and the recent trends revealed in the interpretation of the concept: the move from static and feebly interactive employability concepts to dynamic, strongly interactive ones.

Part 2 will deal with the content of measures for employability promotion and will examine the problems arising from their implementation. In this context, a brief analysis will be made of a tool recently devised in the United States, "profiling," which aims to classify individuals according to their employability needs.

Part 3 will expand the debate by examining the sort of interaction and responsibility that should be developed in the labor markets concerning the supply of jobs. Practices such as "workfare," collective bargaining and social partners will be discussed, and a comparison will be drawn between two key concepts: "making work pay" (OECD) and "making transitions pay" (in the perspective of the "transitional markets").

Employability, a Brief Assessment of Its History and Leading Concepts

A Midway Point between Theories and Practices

Understood as the ability to obtain and to preserve a paid job (salaried or not salaried), employability is not a theoretical notion inserted into a network of explanatory connections or of explicit, univocal and stable standards. Rather, it is a matter of identifying the problems and priorities linked to the actions of persons and institutions involved in the access to work and employment.

From the outset, employability was enmeshed in a set of economic and social, as well as moral, policy concerns. It followed on the old distinction drawn between the valid and the invalid poor, the first of whom received an entirely different treatment from that given the second. The invalid poor are the object of direct material and financial support, while the valid poor have to be put to work. Even today amongst social workers, to qualify a person as unemployable is to channel him/her toward measures and treatments based on financial assistance, with little or no reciprocity required. The person deemed employable, on the other hand, comes under labor market policies.

The term employability was initially operational and laden with concrete stakes, as well as with collective representations. It consigns employability to a network of more or less coherent concepts that fall midway between daily routines and more abstract schemes. Thus, it carries somewhat implicit meanings which often need to be spelled out and may be misleading from a more theoretical point of view, i.e., they may be attributed to several divergent causes.

This intermediate position also makes employability flexible; it has in the course of time accommodated different contents, however with few possibilities of accumulating experiences and developments, since the content itself may differ according to the authors or the trends. These experiences and developments are themselves miscellaneous and have scarcely been mentioned in the overall discussion.

The complexity of this concept ensues, as does the need to synthesize, at the least, the different main versions of employability in preparation for a more decisive analysis.

Seven Main Concepts

The outcome of several historical studies is that at least seven successive versions of the employability concept have been developed in the course of the twentieth century, each with its definition, its statistical reflection and its operational consequences.

In the study mentioned in the introduction in this section, these various versions have been identified and given a name to differentiate them from one another. The names assigned are intended to facilitate a discussion of the whole group and were neither produced nor used by the different authors of any version; the latter have mainly limited their terminology to the word "employability" without seeming to discern that a specific version was in question.

The first version (E1) dates back to the 1900s and persisted, above all, in the United Kingdom and in the United States up to the early 1950s. This version presented employability as a simple dichotomy. A person either was or was not employable, i.e., valid and immediately available on the labor market. The statistical expression of this *dichotomic employability* gradually focused on three criteria which became current in many studies carried out in the United States during the Great Depression of the 1930s: belong to the right age group (between 15 and 64 years of age), not suffer any physical or mental handicap, and not be subject to strong family constraints, such as child-rearing responsibilities for mothers. In this way, people classified as poor were oriented in two different directions: those who were unemployable received emergency social assistance, while those considered employable were assigned to public works projects and returned to the labor market. This system was frequently criticized, on the one hand, because it was established with no thought for the labor market context and, on the other hand, because it did not recognize any degrees between the conditions of employability and unemployability.

The modern versions of the employability concept were born of a second wave of applications and developments during the 1950s and 1960s that extended beyond the Anglo-Saxon framework to include contributions from many other countries and from France in particular. Three very different types of employability have been identified and used by social workers, labor market policy-makers, statisticians and doctors.

The first of these versions was E2, which can be called *socio-medical employability*. Mainly developed by doctors and rehabilitation practitioners and aimed at the handicapped, this version immediately introduced a quantitative scale: one can be more or less employable, and this evaluation constitutes the basis for action to improve employability. Concretely, this consists of ranking a series of items that make up a test of individual employability: the abilities of a more or less handicapped person being graded in different areas that cover physical as well as mental aptitudes and deficiencies (vision, hearing, heart, motor capacity, etc., and also the ability to abstract, to reason, and to take initiative). According to the deficiencies identified, a selection is made of those where intervention is possible so as to cure or to compensate, and a program of action is devised.

This first version was almost immediately succeeded by a more general second version, aimed at the unemployed who have difficulties. In fact, it is possible to introduce in the scale, with different emphases, items relating to social as well as to physical handicaps; thus, attention is focused not only on deficiencies of professional qualifications, but also of mobility and presentation. In this way, a person who does not have a driver's license or has a police record or has been a drug user would be considered less employable. This E3 employability could be called *manpower policy employability*. It measures the distance between the individual's characteristics and the production and acceptability requirements on the labor market. Here again, it is possible to select items on which it is feasible to act (for example, training programs or simply driving lessons or even advice on how to dress).

Versions E2 and E3, developed principally in the United States, are limited by their exclusively individualized focus on the persons being helped to find employment, accepting as immutable both the market conditions and the possible prejudices of employers.

A third variation was developed, especially in France in the 1960s, with a very different approach to the problem, based on a collective dimension. This version, E4, called *flow employability* concentrates on the speed at which a certain group of the unemployed finds work. This is assessed by the proportion within a given group of the jobless—for example, among the unemployed over 50 years of age—

of those who have been without work for more than one year. This statistic of unemployability (rather than of employability) has the advantage of directly relating the situation of the unemployed with that of the labor market (more or less good economic situation, more or less rigid selectivity). From that point, it can be subdivided according to the individual disadvantages of any subgroup of jobless, or of a single unemployed person (a differential employability).

It is quite remarkable that the E2 and E3 versions, on the one hand, and the E4, on the other, were developed separately. In the 1970s, E2 and E3 reached a crisis, principally because their activism on behalf of the workforce seemed to be one-sided by many decision-makers (who considered it more efficient, for example, to introduce greater flexibility in the labor market) and also because the scores made on the different individual employability tests were found to be quite poor forecasts of the success of any given individual on the labor market. At about the same time, during the 1980s, it was the E4 version that came under fire, when massive and lasting unemployment pervaded much of Europe. Indeed, it seemed increasingly demotivating to permanently record a decline in the employability of the jobless and only to assess a collective dimension based mainly on a slowing of the economic growth rate. How then can these persons be helped, if the avenues for rapidly reviving economic activity are blocked? For this reason, French statisticians who were using this system eventually abandoned it.

More recently, during the 1980s and 1990s, a more international third wave, including some contributions from Canada, has proposed three new versions of the employability concept.

Since the late 1970s, a series of American studies have proposed a more neutral statistical definition of employability, E5, which could be called *labor market performance employability*. Taking into account the available statistical information on employment paths, this version establishes for a group or an individual three specified probabilities referred to a defined time lapse: the probability of obtaining one or several jobs, the probable duration of these jobs expressed in hours of work, and the probable salary. By multiplying these three probabilities, a synthetic indicator is obtained for the aptitude of a person or a group for being gainfully employed on the labor market. This measurement is interesting, because it does not focus attention merely on the probability of finding work and because it introduces some minimal indications of the "quality" of a job (duration and salary). It does not propose a priori any link between individual aptitudes, collective situations or the action of economic or social policies and the result in the labor market. It is, in this sense, neutral and can only serve as a retrospective evaluation of one program or another.

This is not the case for two more recent versions developed mainly at the onset of the 1990s: E6, or *initiative employability* and E7, *interactive employability.*

The E6 version underscores the individual responsibility and a person's capacity to trigger a process of accumulation of human capital and social capital around his/her projects. Thus, E6 can be defined as the marketability of cumulative individual skills and can be measured by the breadth of potential or already acquired human capital (knowledge and productive skills, but also learning ability) and by the size and quality of the network of help and support that a person is able to mobilize around himself/herself (social capital). The advantage of this version is its dynamic dimension. However, paradoxically this version favors the characteristics that are closest to the entrepreneurial model, making the most employable person the one who is most able to benefit from his/her knowledge and connections. Thus, the most employable person is the one who creates employment. In this strongly optimistic and individualistic model, one seems far removed from the problems of many, if not most, persons who are seeking work. In terms of policies to be followed, priority should be placed on promoting lifelong learning, improved information about the labor market and its greater flexibility.

It is the last version, E7, which reintroduces the interactive and collective dimensions. Starting from a 1994 Canadian definition, employability can be seen as "the relative capacity of an individual to achieve meaningful employment given the interaction between personal characteristics and the labour market." The statistical reflection, then, is a set of statistical profiles that will connect the individual traits and paths to the circumstances and trends of the labor market. The main operational consequences are the activation of labor market policies such as those mentioned in the introduction to this section, along with the promotion of multidimensional, negotiated approaches.

Some Elements of Interpretation

Within the framework of this document, it is not possible to develop the complex connections between the different versions of employability and economic theories.[2] No single version can be linked directly to one identifiable theory. For example, versions E2, E3, and E6 can to some degree be related to the theory of human capital, but it would be necessary then to complete that connection with a theory on the imperfect adjustments in the labor market, whether there is salary rigidity and/or active job-seeking and mobility in behavior. Similarly, the E4 version refers to "Keynesian employability" without this reference being univocal.

What appears relatively clear is the contrast between the two waves, that of the 1960s and that of the 1980-90s. In fact, the concepts developed during the 1960s stem from two radically different points—one is individual and the other collective—and they do not confront one another at any point. The efforts to adapt the workforce to the labor market assume that the latter can absorb them, and the macro circumstances create an impasse for individual initiatives.

These concepts are barely interactive and quite static in certain regards. They essentially identify collective or individual deficits, in order to attempt to reduce them. This implies setting a stable reference point of "normality" corresponding to employment, which is never to be questioned, and reasoning on the basis of a fixed aim: finding a job.

What appears as a major characteristic of recent developments (leaving aside E5 employability, which is unbiased) is quite the opposite: the emergence of interactive and dynamic approaches. The potential of employability is thus considered in relation to a given context, be it individual networks of "social capital" that may expand or, more generally, changing labor market conditions.

Through this succession of various versions of employability, a gradual learning process may be observed. However, a number of uncertainties remain.

Promoting Employability

Adapting to Market Requirements and the Role of Local Conditions

Considering in substance the measures being applied at the turn of the twentieth century to promote employability, one finds that the measures are not, in fact, innovative but have been given a new slant. Labor market policies (unemployment benefits, placement and information, training and employment grants or subsidies) are indeed well known, timeworn tools. Making employability a priority means essentially developing so-called "active" measures or, in other words, those that do not aim solely to bolster income, but are rather *tailor-made measures designed to have a preventive effect.*

Thus, the *European Employment Strategy* in its chapter on employability sets out three measurable objectives:

- Member states must ensure that their young unemployed are offered a new start before reaching six months of unemployment, either in the form of training, retraining, job experience, employment or other measures aimed at improving their employability.

- They must act likewise for unemployed adults before reaching 12 months of unemployment by offering any of the above-mentioned measures or by accompanying individual vocational guidance.

- Lastly, member states must substantially increase the proportion of recipients of active measures. The target is to gradually reach the average of the three most successful member states and at least 20 percent.

- The British New Deal program launched in 1998 can be seen as a program hinging on this idea.[3] All unemployed youths in a preliminary period lasting up to four months will first be given a grant and individual career guidance regarding employment opportunities both in the private sector and in public service. Young people must then choose from four options: (1) on-the-job training contracts lasting up to six months in the private sector, for which the employer receives a subsidy; (2) temporary jobs in community programs to protect the environment, combined with training, and a salary equivalent to the unemployment benefit plus a small extra payment; (3) jobs in the non-profit-making sector, here too combined with training and a small extra payment; or (4) a one-year, full-time training course, either in further general education or in some vocational branch. Throughout this period, the young New Dealer is accompanied by a mentor or a member of the public employment services.

The two most important innovations are the maintenance of long-term monitoring and the obligation to take one of the four options in order to be eligible for a public subsidy. As has been publicly emphasized, there is no fifth option.

Therefore, through assessments and supervised career planning, pressure is exerted in varying degrees to promote personal mobilization. Also, increased emphasis is laid on the local level, where in fact most of the assistance is provided, either by resorting to the social and professional networks in which the unemployed person is integrated or by facilitating his/her access to other private or public networks.

Often the link between efforts to promote employability and aspirations for a greater earning capacity is neither simple nor unambiguous. Granted practices involving employment subsidies imply lowering the cost of labor in order to make it more attractive for the employers, but they can have very different effects in various cases. Some subsidies lower the cost of labor so as to protect the net wages for the workers, whereas others aim (and in principle achieve this aim) to force workers to lower their expectations, pitting subsidies/benefits, on the one hand, against subsidies/flexibility, on the other.

Furthermore, it should be noted that practices involving improved training for workers while keeping their income expectations unchanged implicitly boil down to salary losses. In general, measures fostering employability can be designed to encourage moderate salary demands.

The trend is set to adapt to market requirements both in terms of types of qualifications offered and in terms of salary expectations. It focuses mainly on "micro policies" which rely heavily on local input. As a result, decentralized public employment services must be able to develop and use optimally a range of diverse services responding to individually identified needs.

Components and Dilemmas of Employability

In an initial phase, the implementation of a single employability measure may clearly be considered. Such a measure may well be assessed on its cost efficiency as viewed by the decision-makers, i.e., if its benefits (savings for the unemployment insurance, additional income for the workers, etc.) outweigh the cost of the measure. Many studies have been carried out to assess this point,[4] which reveal a wide variety of levels of efficiency, seldom spectacular, of the range of "active" labor market policy measures. These suggest that often the mechanisms that are adapted to local circumstances and tailor-made are (slightly) more efficient than the others. The issue then is how to implement such trends on a major scale.

A number of dilemmas appear which are well known to the public authorities and which crop up frequently in relation to employability.

- The first dilemma lies in the selection of recipients to be given priority in implementing the measures designed to improve employability.

Within a set group, the decision-makers (employment agency officials, social workers, etc.) spontaneously tend to help those who are already most employable, as this is the surest way to achieve visible and rapid results at minimum cost. Usually, to counteract this, priority groups are targeted, but the same distortion may reappear in subgroups established in this fashion.

- The *second* dilemma is that of the spillover effects. One solution to this problem is to distribute resources as equally as possible among a variety of different groups, in the hope that this sprinkling technique will be both positive and cumulative. In some way, the successes would, by a momentum effect, "draw" the less efficient ones into employment. Clearly this strategy, which leads certain public employment agencies to try to increase their share of attributed jobs whatever they may be, has inherent contradictions, since the reputation acquired by finding jobs for the most employable bears no favorable effects on the less employable, who once again remain on the sidelines.

- The *third* dilemma resides in the choice between preventive and curative action. In the long term, this dilemma should disappear. If prevention is successful, then curative action should be gradually phased out. However, in the short term, the problem remains of how better to distribute the efforts. This may lead the decision-makers to discourage the least employable job-seekers in order to avoid investing resources in categories of workers whose chances of being hired again are deemed slim.

- The *fourth* dilemma, doubtless the main area under consideration, is the issue of the desired quality of job access. Should job-seekers be "rushed" back into employment as soon as possible, regardless of the low salary, poor qualifications and uncertainty of employment and working conditions that the job in question may offer? Or would it be better to favor more demanding measures in terms of the content of training and of qualifications and to delay the re-entry to the job market? This contradiction was described systematically by opposing "employability access" to "employability performance."[5]

    An illustration of these difficulties is to be found in the rotation job-seekers are subjected to, between unstable poor-quality jobs and relapses into unemployment. This is known as the "revolving door" phenomenon: access to employment has proven neither satisfactory nor lasting.

- One *final* dilemma emerges when considering local development. Such a policy may indeed generate a large quantity of flexible and dependent jobs or, on the contrary, pave the way for a growth pattern with fewer but more stable jobs to offer.

Ultimately, employment development policies seem to rely on three interdependent sets of choices: guaranteeing access to jobs, preventing it, and opening opportunities for improving qualifications. These are three components in a sense: the measures vary although they may be mixed, and the groups that will receive differentiated treatment must undergo a selection process. But when is that selection legitimate, accepted and socially and economically efficient?

"Profiling": A Tool under Review[6]

Since the mid-1990s, experiments have been conducted in the United States in which the technique known as "profiling" was seen as a potential element of solutions to the various implementation difficulties described above.[7] The technique involves establishing at the local level (in a local employment agency, for example) a permanent priority ranking system of potential clients for an active labor market policy, with a view to provide them, in addition to the standard services for the unemployed, with intensive and tailor-made "activation" programs.

The ranking is applied to persons enrolling for unemployment benefits and who are thus eligible for employment services and a variety of active "measures." Based on the person's characteristics (qualifications, former trade, job experience) and on the variables of the local job catchment area (unemployment rate, number of jobs created in the area, etc.), a statistical model is drawn up in order to estimate the time the person is likely to remain under unemployment benefits. The ranking is designed to place those who, according to statistical probability assessed at the outset, are likely to spend the longest in the unemployment insurance system at the top and the following ranks in a decreasing order.

There is thus no absolute level (seen as desirable or not) but only an order of priority. The limited resources available to public service employment agency agents are thus attributed to those whose needs are considered greatest and then down the scale until they are exhausted. Hence, the line between those who are granted special assistance and those who are not is perfectly arbitrary. It is drawn in the middle of a continuous scale and is determined by the resources available to the employment services.

It should be noted that "profiling" provides no guidance as to the type of measure that would be advisable for any given category of job-seeker. Once the ranking has been established, job-seekers are invited to a series of individual interviews. On that basis, and on the strength of their expertise, employment officers design, according to available means, a personalized program of actions suited to the person's individual needs. It should be mentioned that if the job-seeker fails to appear at the interviews he is struck off the unemployment benefits roster. As is often the case, efforts directed at those whose chances of employment are most remote also afford an opportunity to put their motivation to the test and to exert some pressure on them. This is an element known as the "labor rejection" factor of employability.

The cost-benefit studies carried out in the United States demonstrate the cost-effectiveness of such mechanisms. The dollars invested in the implementation of the statistical program are covered by the shorter average period unemployed persons spend under the unemployment benefit scheme. There are even net benefits, significant though not spectacular. Added advantages are obtained when various actors must coordinate their efforts (for example, from the private and the public sectors, from training and from employment agencies). As this method affords an estimate of the intensity of each person's needs, it becomes easier to rally around common priorities.

"Profiling" has become a general practice in the United States, and its application to other population groups is under way—specifically poor, young, single mothers who are being channeled towards employment. This technique, however, has given rise to many a heated debate in Europe. Objections were first raised on ethical and political grounds. In a culture based on equality among citizens, it seems shocking to attribute to a person at a given time in his or her history a personalized objective ranking of his/her chances of finding a job, a rank that determines a difference of treatment in an arbitrary fashion (partially, at least). Furthermore, it is interesting to note that, for ethical and political reasons, the American practice has excluded from the model three personal variables: sex, age and race.[8] These identifying elements would appear to raise fewer problems in Europe, where it would more likely be the actual results of such tests, the establishment and potential dissemination of an arbitrary ranking that runs counter to the principle of equal treatment for all.

Another, probably deeper, problem arises when "profiling" is to be applied in situations in which long-term unemployment rates are very high and the job-seeking population is mixed. It may well be that the periods spent under unemployment insurance coverage (or, on the contrary, the probabilities of being hired or of giving up the search for a job) in the long term do not prove to be stable indicators and that new estimates are required every six months, for example. It may therefore be a mistake to base career guidance, and to recommend a "treatment," on a single personal indicator established once and for all, albeit bearing the context in mind.

Searching for "Active Security"

"Activation" and "Workfare" Short-Term Pressures

The trend towards an "activation" of labor market policies is one of the facts that has rarely been challenged over the past decade. Who indeed would be so bold as to question that it is better to spend public funds on measures fostering employment rather than on unemployment benefits?

Nevertheless, the division between "active" and "passive" expenditures, broadly inspired by the successful labor market policies implemented in Scandinavian countries and singularly in Sweden in the 1980s, is not as clear-cut as generally thought. "Passive" would imply that the aim is simply to compensate the jobless for the ill effects of unemployment, whereas "active" would involve actions to improve the match between supply and demand on the labor market. This division, widely popularized by the OECD terminology which classifies and quantifies the elements of labor market policies, is rather vague regarding practices such as "bogus" training courses. These, although they are considered "active," may well turn out to be no more than a "passive" tool. Likewise, a generous benefits program may prove to have "active" effects if it were to facilitate the search for jobs.

In any event, most developed countries have focused their efforts on cutting back their expenditures on benefits and increasing the resources allocated to employment services, training and grant programs. Is the aim to reproduce the Swedish model, with all the concerted mechanisms to promote mobility, collective bargaining and the relatively low salary differentials? The answer is clearly no. The following *hypothesis* is easy to posit: the main cause for the trend towards "activation" certainly resides in trying to improve the management of ever-increasing budgets, which are intolerable for certain groups of taxpayers. As unemployment becomes more permanent, costly and devoid of any chances for rapid improvement, the persistence of the situation in itself raises new demands—for instance, that the recipients of such benefits and various forms of aid pay back the community, in part or in total, for the efforts made.

A wide variety of "activation" measures can be brought to the fore. They may range from ambitious and structured programs geared to offer the jobless new opportunities to simple restrictive practices designed to limit the number of those eligible for unemployment benefits or to cut back the duration of such benefits. Actions can focus exclusively, or separately, on either "passive" or "active" programs in order to limit the former and promote the latter or, on the contrary, an attempt can be made to combine both types of action. "Make Work Pay," a slogan coined by the OECD, sums up the intent, when beyond labor market policies the aim is to alter the link with taxation and allied policies, which may have an encouraging or dissuasive effect on employment. The objective is to eliminate all public provisions which may hamper job creation or to reduce the financial incentive for the jobless.

The vital question thus becomes: What kind of time frame should be set for applying these reciprocity or restitution criteria?

Practices known as "workfare," implemented and discussed in the United States, are the most systematic attempt to attribute an intrinsic value to work and to restrict incentives and disincentives to individual cases. Such practices introduce a set of programs to find jobs, to provide training for requalification and to reintegrate jobseekers into the labor market, including actions described previously, but these are complemented by non-skilled low-paid forced labor activities. These activities clearly contain a punitive element. They are designed to show the able-bodied unemployed that society expects them to reciprocate immediately. If efforts are made to help them, they must pay back society straight away, or at least very soon, either by finding another job quickly or by means of a more or less humiliating contribution.

Part of this overall approach is reflected in the trend towards decentralization, towards "local" assessment of needs and abilities. Another component is placing the bulk of the burden of adjusting to prevalent labor market conditions on the individual job-seeker.

These practices based on solidarity with strings attached are the repressive aspect of the short-term pressures in favor of employment and of greater individual employability. It is worth mentioning that Latin countries, which are most often very far from imposing such criteria, are not necessarily more accommodating to persons who are difficult to hire and who depend on social aid or minimum revenue programs. The formal statement of citizenship along with the requirement to actively look for a job that may well not exist is hardly better than the obligation to do some work.

From this brief debate, it may be concluded that what is questionable is not the reciprocity criterion. It is without a shadow of a doubt the basis on which life in society and social integration is rooted. The issue at stake is the time frame in which it can be implemented, i.e., in the short, the medium or the long term. Another issue lies in determining who will provide the bases for such reciprocity, i.e., who will be the participants in laying its foundations.

Negotiating Mobilities

At this juncture, one should step back to encompass a larger perspective. Employability promotion measures are often portrayed as active adjustments to labor market requirements. However, the opportunities afforded by such measures rely on the workforce's mobility. The clearest example of this interdependence can be seen in "job rotation" practices such as the Danish leave system.

It should be noted that in Denmark three types of leave have been tried out: parental leave, sabbatical leave, and time off for training purposes. One possible case in point would be to organize a replacement contract with financial support from the state. This would involve hiring a previously trained long-term unemployed person to replace the person on leave. The substitution ends when the titular employee returns to his/her position. But the end result of this to and fro is primarily that an unemployed person has been restored to employability. Indeed, the person involved has been "rehabilitated" and can prove in his future job applications that he/she has recent job experience and references. Two aims are thus fulfilled: job sharing which ensues from any leave with a replacement mechanism, and restoration of employability or, in other words, "mainstreaming" of the labor market.

Therefore, as many countries are tempted to call the range of active measures they have included in their labor market policies "employability insurance," this being the second tier of the unemployment insurance system (since the first is composed of "passive" mechanisms to compensate the unemployed), then a third tier is required to complete the system which could be named "mobility insurance." This would include a variety of mobility rights to which workers are entitled, whether or not they hold a job, i.e., the right to take leave, to training, to accumulate time-capital. In very general terms, these rights should be as homogeneous as possible and be subjected to decentralized negotiations, in order to match developments to needs as closely as possible and to offer credible opportunities to the jobless.[9] Only if this prerequisite is fulfilled will the second tier avoid the repressive and bureaucratic pitfalls described above. Within this broader perspective, "transitional markets" are construed as systematic endeavors to deploy interactive E 7 employability.[10]

Without going into detail, it should be pointed out that "transitional markets" are a trend of labor market reforms designed to apply decentralized negotiations systematically to all types of labor mobility: mobility within and around the job market. Hence, they would include switches from full-time to part-time employment and back, as well as community-centered part-time work, study leave, groupings of employers, etc. The underlying idea is to foster joint financing involving the social partners along with local authorities, community organizations, etc. These should enable "transitions" to be organized efficiently so that temporary jobs can be combined in variable proportions with periods in remunerated employment and periods devoted to useful community work.

To a certain extent, labor market policies amount to unilateral state-run projections of "transitional markets." Such "transitions" are intrinsically neither good nor bad; they may turn either way, i.e., they may ensure independent career development or, on the contrary, lead to declassification or marginalization. Major corporations have specialized in offering their best employees constant career progression. Now the challenge resides in avoiding that the measures designed for the less-favored workers (as part of labor market policies) confine them to a "loser's track." The dotted career pattern should rather be used as a tool to achieve greater homogeneity in the labor market.

One cannot go into the pros and cons of the implementation of "transitional markets." These still remain a set of proposals requiring further experimentation and assessment. It is noteworthy that the least employable job-seekers are the core recipients of publicly financed transitional measures, while other categories are found eligible for projects financed by private companies and the social partners.

Next comes the question of incentives. To develop an open network of "transitional" measures requires that these be attractive both in terms of guaranteed income and of future positions to which they give access (in the paid job as well as in the non-commercial activity). Thus, "making transitions pay" becomes the name of the game, one that is decidedly to be played on a relatively level field in terms of salaries and labor market conditions.

Regarding the variety of incentives and disincentives to be considered both for individual workers and for companies,[11] it is worth mentioning that certain types of solutions are emerging for the desirable forms of reciprocity.

At one end of the spectrum, the direct or indirect adjustment to the prevailing labor market forces is to be found, with its proclivity to inequality and the erosion of the protection offered to ordinary workers. This is known as "workfare" or "making work pay."

At the opposite end is the claim to unconditional income, as it is held that each person's contribution in terms of work must be considered over his/her life span. This leads directly to Universal Benefits or Citizens' Income. Is it a choice between the short term, which could become instantaneous, versus the life-long horizon?

In both cases, what seems shocking is the lack of interest for the actors, the institutions and the shifting jobs which interact on the labor market. All these factors are supposed to work together smoothly.

However, with "transitional markets" in view, such straightforward coordination seems rather unlikely. It may prove sensible to complement salary negotiations with negotiations on mobility issues, so as to multiply the margins for adjustment between supply and demand. This interactive scenario is to a certain extent the middle of the road, half way between the immediate demand of reciprocity and the indefinite deferral of this demand. In this scenario, temporary positions can be offered to job-seekers throughout their lives, while the reciprocity will build up over the successive negotiated sequences. But this is not only a middle-of-the-road solution; it implies that "active security" is achieved through a collective choice of structure which enables each individual to design and then manage his/her own personal and professional project.

The contrast between "passive protection" and "active security" gains a new dimension. At the turn of the millenium, research on unemployment and on active labor market policies led to recording the erosion of traditional forms of worker protection, at least concerning the more integrated workers, those who follow set career paths and benefit from guarantees provided by big corporations that set up so-called "internal markets."

Therefore, one might imagine re-instituting those guarantees in order to establish anew groups of well-unionized and defended workers. However, this option, though perfectly feasible in some instances, proves difficult to extend to most cases, especially in an environment subjected by and large to the development of flexible companies organized in networks or in "profit-making centers." Such a solution might even turn out to be counterproductive if a relatively small group of privileged workers were to be isolated, while the others would be submitted to growing, even cumulative, insecurity. The stabilization base for workers thus becomes too narrow. The function of "transitional markets" would thus be to enlarge the stabilization margin for workers, granting them new rights, individual rights collectively organized.

Referring one last time to the many versions of employability, with no pretense at integrating them all, it would appear that the perspective afforded by the "transitional markets" provides the best opportunities to mobilize and combine them.

E1, the first version, was the only one to be explicitly gender oriented and to take into account the limitations to being employed, or not, that derive from the family situation. Despite its simplistic nature, this has undoubted merit. Another limiting factor is the acceptance of these restrictions as immutable, while collective choices can reorient them: those mentioned in this section, not only by creating new margins for maneuver for mothers, but also by reshaping careers (through the use of "transitions") and by organizing the involvement of the fathers.

A new balance is clearly introduced as well in reviewing the two activist versions of the employability concepts, E2 and E3, aimed at bringing employment opportunities closer to the physically and socially handicapped: the credibility of the rehabilitation agendas is reflected as much by the way in which employment supply and demand are organized as by the support policies envisaged.

The E4 employability-flow concept is given serious consideration for introducing growth dynamics as well as anti-discriminatory concerns. In contrast to this exclusively collective point of view, the "transitional markets" seek to organize and activate individual initiatives. This factor brings them closer to the set of three recent versions.

While E5 remains neutral, it serves as the measure of success for the different "transitions," and it is evident that the interactive version E7 is preferred by the "transitional markets" over the E6, which is deemed too one-sided. They do accept, nevertheless, the validity of careers based on the accumulation of resources and personal learning.

This synthesis can in no way be construed as an instrumental integration. The challenges of implementing employability still lie ahead, and a great deal of work will be needed before the potential and the limits of the "transitional markets"[12] can be assessed.

Conclusions

The purpose of this brief deliberation was to introduce a more systematic discussion of the concept of employability by presenting elements of information and argumentation that are normally found only in a scattered fashion. Employability is still today a sensitive issue in some countries, where it is thought that developing jobs is preferable to developing employability and that emphasizing employability enhances the temptation to charge the jobless for the costs of adapting to the labor market.

In the context of the present upturn in the employment rate, especially in Europe, strong pressures will be felt to promote unilateral versions of employability, since opportunities to get back to work will be more numerous and the labor market policies effort will seem less urgent. This attitude pays scant attention to the likelihood that such opportunities will be reserved for the workers judged, rightly or wrongly, to be the most fit, leaving aside the long-term unemployed.

This is not to say that there is no point in promoting individual initiatives, but it would be more just, socially speaking, and also more efficient to integrate them into a group of initiatives and collective structures that create a credible, socially controllable scope of action. In this section, all the limitations of an overly unilateral vision of employability have been identified. The importance of taking explicit and negotiated account of the aspects of interactive employability is also emphasized.

Other institutions take part in this process, e.g., the various systems for child care, parental leave, salary savings accounts, capital-risk networks, community service or volunteer jobs. Basically, it is a way of redressing power relations in the labor market, so often slanted in favor of the employer in a context of weakened unions whose very legitimacy is under threat.

It thus becomes possible to follow collectively the changes in salary relations, while leaving open areas for individual freedom. This can be accomplished by making each worker a more aware and more independent organizer of the succession of activities and commitments that, combined, constitute his/her working life. Would that not be a good up-to-date definition for the word employability?

Notes

1. B. Gazier (ed.), *Employability: Concepts and Policies*, European Commission, Employment and Social Affairs/IAS, Berlin, 1999.
2. Ibid., pp. 54-61.
3. Cf. J. Philpott's presentation in Gazier (ed.), op. cit., pp. 97-120, and N. Meager in this publication (ch. 5).
4. See, for example, G. Schmid, J. O'Reilly, and K. Schöman (eds.), *Handbook of Labour Market Policy and Evaluation*, Edward Elgar, 1966, which dwells at length on the difficulties and methodological premises of assessment studies in labor market policies.
5. J. Philpott, op. cit.
6. For more detailed information, see H. Rudolph in this publication (ch. 2).
7. See study by R. Eberts in B. Gazier (ed.), 1999, op. cit., pp. 121-146.
8. Such variables are easily deduced from past job experience, type of training and industry, etc.
9. See G. Schmid, B. Gazier, and S. Flechtner in Gazier (ed.), 1999, op. cit., pp. 268-297.
10. See G. Schmid, "Le plein emploi, est-il encore possible? Les marchés du travail 'transitoires' en tant que nouvelle stratégie dans les politiques d'emploi," in *Travail et Emploi*, 1995, no. 65, pp. 5-17, for the initial descriptions; B. Gazier, "Ce que sont les marchés transitionnels," in J.C. Barbier and J. Gautié (eds.), *Les politiques de l'emploi en Europe et aux E.U.*, 1998, for a more in-depth study.
11. On this point, see B. Gazier, "L'articulation justice locale/justice globale, le cas des "marchés transitionnels du travail," *Revue économique*, May 2000, forthcoming.
12. As concerns some major implementation problems, see B. Gazier, 2000.

2

Profiling as an Instrument for Early Identification of People at Risk of Long-Term Unemployment

Helmut Rudolph

Introduction

"Improving employability" is the first of the pillars in the *European Employment Strategy* defined in the 1998 European Union *Employment Guidelines*:

A key element of the employability pillar is the recognition of the need for early intervention, before individuals become long-term unemployed, and the provision of help which is customized and targeted to individual needs.(...)

(...The) member states will develop preventive and employability-oriented strategies, building on the early identification of individual needs; (...) member states will ensure that:

- every unemployed young person is offered a new start before reaching six months of unemployment, in the form of training, retraining, work practice, a job or other employability measures;

- unemployed adults are also offered a fresh start before reaching 12 months of unemployment by one of the aforementioned means or, more generally, by accompanying individual guidance.

The implementation of this strategy implies a shift of policy orientation from passive support by benefits to active measures of learning, training and work experience. Labour market policy (LMP) measures should focus on early prevention of long-term unemployment and less on cure after unemployed people have lost their connection to the labor market. Monitoring this target should guarantee that but few people remain out of work until they reach the long-term unemployed (LTU) status.

This ambitious objective implies the need for early identification of unemployed persons at high risk of long-term unemployment. It implies as well a reorientation of labor market policy from curative or reactive intervention to preventive activities. Legislation has to open training, job creation or job subsidies for people at an early stage of unemployment. However, budgets for active policies are limited, so that the need arises to define who should receive support at an early stage of unemployment.

A number of countries have experimented with or implemented some kind of profiling to target activities to groups of unemployed in need of support. The quest for early identification outlined in the *Employment Guidelines* and monitored in the National Action Plans (NAPs) will certainly have a mobilizing effect in the development and improvement of profiling instruments.

Profiling: Objectives and Types

Evidence on the effectiveness of active labor market policies (ALMPs) suggests that they should be well targeted to the needs of individual job-seekers and the labor market and that treatment should start as early as possible in the unemployment spell. But offering individual treatment along with early intervention would be very costly. There is thus a premium on accurately identifying job-seekers at risk.[1]

To comply with the EU *Employment Guidelines* for offering a new start to every unemployed person before 12 months of unemployment[2] and to consider the trade-off between a costly early intervention strategy to all job-seekers and the premium for early intervention for those at high risk, one needs a decision rule to define:

- who is in need of job-search support,

- when support will be offered, and

- what kind of support will be made available.

Any *formal procedure* to help in the decision to whom, when, and what kind of preventive intervention should be offered is called *a profiling instrument*. Of course, there are rules for intervention in national labor market law and in ordinances within employment services. For example, conditions like minimum unemployment duration, age limit, insufficient qualification or handicap are outlined in national regulations to define eligibility to specific LMPs. Minimum previous employment, minimum contribution to unemployment insurance (UI) or status as benefit recipient may condition availability of specific support.

Especially long-term unemployment as a precondition for participation implies a rule that some type of support will only be offered after a waiting period and excludes a program as a preventive strategy. Therefore, regulations often include clauses to open programs under specific conditions. Thus, only the most obvious factors to characterize a person in need of support are laid down in the regulations. They finally leave the decision of when and to whom this kind of support should be offered open to the discretion of the local employment offices.

Therefore, profiling should incorporate a thorough assessment of the risks a person is likely to face during job search. It should be systematic to all or a well-defined group of persons so that no one is excluded from services and support that may be useful to him/her, and, if used as an instrument for preventive strategies, profiling should be used at an early stage of unemployment. As profiling is not a self-contained objective, there should be procedures to channel the unemployed to appropriate services and programs of support to bring them into employment or increase their employability.

According to the objectives of profiling, there are different elements to characterize profiling instruments. These elements include the kind of risk assessed through profiling, the method to define the risk, and the timing when the risk is assessed.

The Kind of Risk Assessed

The EU *Employment Guidelines* obviously put the emphasis on the prevention of LTU. Therefore, the most obvious way for profiling would be to assess the probability of becoming LTU. An alternative is to evaluate the chances of finding work within 12 months. The sophisticated difference is shown by the fact that not all persons who leave unemployment take up a job. Many withdraw from the labor force, e.g., through early retirement or by participation in training measures. Thus, the availability of LMP or early retirement schemes affects the evaluation of risk directly and should be taken into account when designing the profiling instrument.

Other kinds of risk assessment may be defined. In the United States, with low levels of LTU and scarce funds for LMP, profiling is based on the risk of exhausting benefits. Canada is targeting the cost and employment effectiveness of programs given the clients' characteristics.

The Method of Profiling

For the formal assessment of risks through profiling, several methods (sometimes combined) can be used. Until recently, most employment services have accepted the judgment of placement officers as to whether a job-seeker should be offered some kind of support for integration. As all individual circumstances have to be considered, some form of judgment obviously has to be incorporated into the risk assessment. As an ad-hoc judgment may include a number of factors not obvious to others, there is a problem that different officers may come to different conclusions. This problem can be overcome through more formalized criteria of judgment.

Judgment-based profiling is then a formalized and standardized procedure to evaluate the risk of a client by the employment services. It should provide a systematic check-up of a client's strengths, weaknesses and handicaps of importance for re-employment under the current labor market situation.

Model-based predictions of LTU risk systematically evaluate past labor market performance according to the characteristics incorporated in a statistical model. The models are fitted to past data of individuals for whom it was already known if they had become LTU. Comparing the predicted and observed inflow to LTU can check the prediction quality of the model. As LTU risk is changing with changing labor market conditions, there may be a need to regularly adapt the model, say, on a yearly basis.[3]

Model-based profiling attributes a risk score to an individual based on his/her characteristics, i.e., all individuals with the same characteristics will obtain the same risk score. Nevertheless, people are different and may have different properties not measurable or not included in the model. Therefore, there is a danger that even a good model may not predict individual perspectives sufficiently.

In judgment-based profiling, it may be complicated to weigh correctly the factors considered to influence the individual risk. In model-based profiling, not all relevant individual factors are available for evaluation. Thus, it is straightforward to combine both approaches in two-stage profiling instruments.

A two-stage profiling instrument would yield a risk score for groups of job-seekers from a statistical model that then is corrected for individual strengths and weaknesses by a judgment of the individual case. By doing so, one hopes to minimize classification errors attached to all predictions (see Figure 2.1 and Table 2.1).

Figure 2.1 shows the stylized distribution of risk scores from a fictive model to predict LTU. The thin and thick curves give model scores of people who did not or did become LTU, respectively. If it were decided to give treatment to all with a score of above s_0, most of the LTU would be targeted. But there are some people who became LTU with scores below s_0 who would have been denied treatment (dark shaded area). Also, some people with scores above s_0 (light shaded area) who did not need treatment were offered assistance.

If the decision rule were "offer treatment to all with a score over s_2," intervention would be channelled only to people in need, but in

Figure 2.1
Risk Score of Profiling Model

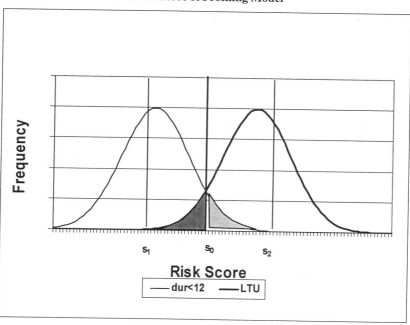

fact a majority of the LTU would not receive treatment. Only the most obvious cases would profit from preventive action. If the decision rule were "offer treatment to all with a score over s_1," all LTU would receive treatment together with a majority of short-term unemployed. This implies considerable dead weight and wasted funds.

The outcome of profiling appears as presented in Table 2.1:

Table 2.1
Prediction of LTU

	LTU: no	LTU: yes	
score ≤ s	c_1	e_1	where $c_1+e_1+c_2+e_2=100$; percentages of classified cases
score > s	e_2	c_2	$c_1 + c_2$ correctly classified; $e_1 + e_2$ misclassified

The problem is to minimize the misclassification $e_1 + e_2$. Different costs are related to the two types of errors: denied treatment with the costly consequences of LTU in the case of e_1, costly treatment not needed in the case of e_2.

A profiling instrument will yield good results if there is little misclassification or, statistically speaking, if the intersection area under the two curves is small.

The Time for Profiling

Profiling is the attempt to classify people into groups with high- or low-duration risk. When a person becomes unemployed, no one knows how long he or she will take to find a job. It is only after a year that one is able to decide whether the category of LTU applies. The later the profiling is carried out, the fewer the number of cases to undergo profiling and the better the chances to avoid misclassification. But the later profiling is applied, the more time is lost for prevention and more money has to be spent on benefits. This shows that timing of profiling and of the decision for support is important for the cost and effectiveness of performance.

Good timing depends on the sorting process during unemployment, i.e., sorting job-seekers into short and long spells of job search. Becoming unemployed and finding a job are two highly selective processes in the interaction of employers and workers, employment services and educational institutions. Economic decisions on cost and productivity mix with institutional and legal regulations. An individual's professional qualification matters as well as his/her so-

Figure 2.2
The Stayer Curve

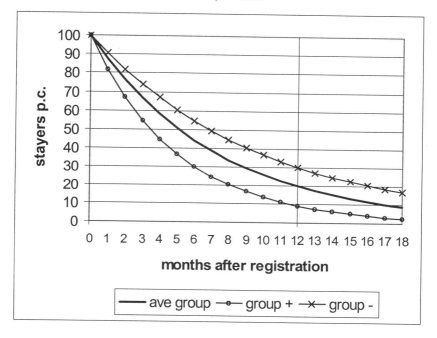

cial behavior and adaptability. These factors are supposed to influence who becomes unemployed (inflow risk) and who stays unemployed (duration risk). Or is it mere hazard that determines who gets a job offer and who does not?

Consider a cohort of newly registered unemployed during a week of, say, 100 persons composed in a representative way. If they are followed with their job search, it can be seen that they gradually leave the register through job entries or by withdrawing their registration (see Figure 2.2). Only a part of them, about 20 percent for example under current German labor market conditions, will stay for more than a year and become long-term unemployed. A stayer curve like that depicted in the figure can be observed.

The level of the stayer curve after 12 months is better known as the inflow rate to long-term unemployment. This measure is currently introduced in EU member states to monitor the effectiveness of preventive policies against LTU. First results from National Action Plans of this indicator are shown in Table 2.2 (col. 3).

Table 2.2
Unemployment Rate, LTU and LTU Inflow Rate in EU Countries, 1999

Country	Unemployment rate	Long-term unemployment	LTU inflow rate adults
	1)	2)	3)
Belgium	8.6	60.5	35.0
Germany	8.9	51.7	16.7
Denmark	5.1	20.5	4.0 (1998)
Greece (1998)	10.8	54.9	n.a.
Spain	15.7	46.3	7.9 (?)
Finland	11.7	22.7	10.6
France	12.1	38.7	15.9 (?)
Ireland	5.7	55.9	n.a.
Italy	11.7	61.4	n.a.
Luxembourg	2.4	32.3	13.8
Netherlands	3.6	43.5	26.0 (?)
Austria	4.7	31.7	1.0
Portugal	4.6	41.2	23.8
Sweden	7.6	29.5	15.0
United Kingdom	6.2	29.8	11.0

1)   EUROSTAT: Standardized unemployment rate, *Labour Force Survey 1999*.
2)   EUROSTAT: Percent of unemployed with a duration of 12 months and above, *Labour Force Survey 1999*.
3)   European Commission: proportion of unemployed who stayed unemployed for more than 12 months of those who became unemployed in 1998 (adults 25 years and older). Compilation from National Action Plans.
(?):   Approximations or data deficiencies.
Note: The inflow rate to LTU is a new indicator and depends on the way national registers of unemployed are administered. Therefore, availability of comparable data has to be improved. The measurement of duration in the *Labour Force Survey* and national unemployment registers may vary.

If the duration of job search were determined by mere hazard, a distinction between more or less employable groups would be in vain. But if "more employable" groups of persons who exit unemployment more rapidly could be determined from "less employable" persons right from the start, stayer curves could be observed with different slopes and different proportions entering long-term unemployment.

Experience, based on statistics, shows that there is a sorting in the speed that exits occur related to a number of characteristics of the labor market and of the individual. The different unemployment duration leads to a changing composition of the initial entry cohort. If at entry a cohort were composed at a 50:50 ratio of less or more employable people,[4] after 12 months the ratio in the above example would be 30:5. The sorting leaves a higher proportion of less employable persons in the stock of LTU. This effect is called the segmentation of unemployment by duration.

This segmentation is measured either by group-specific proportions of long-term unemployed in the stock of unemployed or by group-specific inflow rates to LTU.[5] The LTU inflow rate describes the group-specific risk of becoming long-term unemployed.

The stayer curve also demonstrates that early identification has to deal with a far higher number of cases than identification after three or six months when a high percentage of persons from the entry cohort has already left unemployment. The proportion of those actually becoming LTU increases as time passes, and the chances to correctly identify this group should improve.

Therefore, waiting until the sorting process has worked and the stayer curve has dropped almost to the level of the LTU inflow rate would yield good targeting of the LTU and low misclassification but would not leave much time for prevention. It would gamble away the premium on early identification.

Thus, depending on the predictive quality of the profiling instrument, one has to decide whether the instrument should be applied at an early stage. It can be applied at entry of unemployment (early profiling) or after a waiting period (time-dependent profiling) of three or six months. Then, the more employable group and the fortunate ones from less employable groups have left unemployment. Assessment by profiling may be repeated during the unemployment period, either periodically or whenever new information to be taken into account becomes obvious, e.g., after a training measure.

Influencing Factors of the Risk of LTU

Profiling as a formal instrument evaluates risks or defines the appropriate support for an individual. The sorting process in the labor market, however, is not exclusively determined by character-istics of the individual, but foremost by the availability of employ-ment opportunities in the regional or qualification-related labor mar-ket. Inflow into LTU varies with the unemployment rate.

If the intention of profiling is to predict LTU, then the most im-portant factors correlated with LTU should be incorporated in the instrument.

Factors of the Labor Market

The local unemployment rate seems to be the most important vari-able for measuring the inflow rate to LTU. As labor markets may be partitioned into profession, qualification or industry-related segments, variables to assess different employment possibilities of the segments should be available.

The performance of industries in the region is crucial for the de-mand for labor. An example for the relation between the unemploy-ment rate and the inflow rate to LTU is shown in Figure 2.3 for German employment offices in 1999. The West and East German regions are marked separately. Both show a positive correlation of the two indicators. It is striking that East German unemployment rates are nearly twice the West German average, but LTU inflow rates compare well with regions in West Germany of above-average unemployment rates. The simple explanation is that there are con-siderable more funds for active policy available in the eastern re-gions, which are used at least to interrupt unemployment.

Figure 2.3
LTU Inflow Rate by Unemployment Rate for German Regions 1999

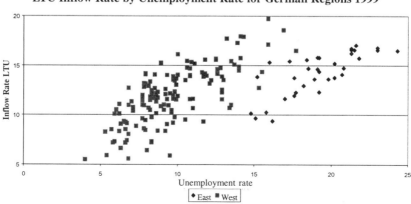

For Germany, the regional or the local unemployment rate is, after age, the most powerful variable to explain the inflow into LTU.[6] The incorporation of the local unemployment rate should therefore improve risk assessment.

Statistical Characteristics of the Individual

Numerous articles have been published to explain unemployment duration or long-term unemployment in different countries through statistical variables available from surveys or administrative data. The most relevant variables seem to be age, qualification, gender, health status and nationality/ethnic origin.[7] Others may be related to work history (experience, previous unemployment, previous wage rate, etc.) or household composition (number of earners in the household, household income, etc.).

The variables are associated with the risk of LTU, as they are supposed to capture differences in the skills and productivity of the worker. In economic theory, they are considered as explaining the "human capital" and the socioeconomic behavior of a worker. Even if they do not determine the skills and productivity of the individual, they constitute "signals" of employability to an employer.

The importance of these variables varies by country and study, sometimes reflecting differences in legislation, sometimes differences of measurement or data quality. In any case, there is no unique set of variables to predict LTU correctly.

Other Characteristics of the Individual

A third group of factors are those related to personal attitudes and psychological characteristics of the individual. They comprise job-search efforts and motivation for work, readiness to adapt to new working conditions and self-consciousness. These factors are harder to measure and therefore more difficult to include into model-based profiling. They generally have to be assessed by judgment during an interview with the unemployed.

Profiling Experiences in Some Countries

Since the 1980s, researchers have investigated data of unemployed individuals to model and explain factors influencing unemployment duration or the risk of LTU. It seems to be straightforward to apply these models to forecast unemployment duration for new entrants and use them as a decision rule for special support. However, statistical models predict the average LTU risk of groups of unemployed according to a set of characteristics, but there is still considerable variation for individuals within each group. While a good model will predict fairly well the proportion of people becoming LTU in a group with given characteristics, it is less obvious that the model will correctly identify the individuals within the group.

A number of countries have experimented with or implemented some kind of profiling instrument. A nationwide profiling for newly registered unemployed or benefit claimants was introduced in the United States and Australia in 1994 and in the Netherlands in 1999. Since 1995 Canada has been testing a tool to determine efficient support to job-seekers. After thorough examination, Great Britain refrained from introducing formal profiling. Germany started a controlled experiment on profiling in three employment offices early in 2000.

The Netherlands: The "Kansmeter"

In January 1999, the employment services in the Netherlands introduced the "Kansmeter" (Chance Meter) as a first instrument to define services suitable for the job-seeker. Services are to be made available according to the client's distance from the labor market.[8] The distance is measured by the probability of taking up a job within a year with or without support. The grouping by the Kansmeter is called "phasing."

The Kansmeter is used at the intake interview and may be reviewed later during unemployment. Based on the job-seeker's answers in a questionnaire and additional information collected during the interview, the placement officer follows an elaborated and standardized decision plan to evaluate a point score of the individual's labor market chances and to determine a measure of the distance from the labor market. The scores from the formal decision plan can be corrected if the placement officer has good reason to believe that they result in misleading perspectives of integration, but he must note down his reasoning. The outcome determines whether the job-seeker is ready for immediate integration (group 1), can be integrated with some kind of assistance (groups 2 and 3) or needs other assistance before LMP measures would become meaningful (group 4).

Groups 2 and 3 will be transferred for further assessment of the individual barriers to take up employment and the type of support needed. A second type of instrument is currently developed to formalize this decision during the "qualifying intake."

Group 4 as well has to undergo a "qualifying intake" to determine the kind of problems and the type of social assistance to cope with these problems.

At the end of the procedure, job-seekers are classified into one of the four groups. The placement officer discusses the result of the measurement and the related prognostics of the LM chances with the client and explains the assistance available. The client has the right to contest the outcome of the grouping and ask for revision by a different service.

The four resulting groups[9] are:

- Group 1: Job-seekers who are ready for immediate integration into the LM: Basic services of placement and information are available to them.

- Group 2: Job-seekers with increased risk of LTU, who with the assistance of some LM measures of less than 12 months have chances to improve their employability; available services: job-search training and qualification.

- Group 3: Job-seekers with high risk of LTU, who need intensive assistance of LM measures of more than a year to improve their employment chances; coordinated integration instruments.

- Group 4: Job-seekers with severe personal handicaps who need support and assistance to arrive at a position where LM measures to improve chances of employment could be meaningful (e.g., drug users or those with psychiatric problems). The placement service does not provide for this group of people, who have no real chance in the labor market and are transferred to special services within communities or social security.

The grouping is not definite, but will be revised during the unemployment period or after measures. In this regard, it should reflect the dynamic process of LM integration.

The formal scores are based on gender, age, level of education, work experience and Dutch or non-Dutch origin. The scores are differentiated according to more than 100 occupations in 18 LM regions from inflow data of unemployed persons in 1993 and 1994.[10]

An evaluation of the handling of the Kansmeter during its first year of implementation has been carried out, and a report is forthcoming. An evaluation of the effectiveness of the grouping to prevent LTU and updating of the regional and occupational scores for job-seekers are planned for the near future.

The United States: The Worker Profiling and Re-employment Services (WPRS)

In November 1993, the United States Congress passed legislation to set up the Worker Profiling and Re-employment Services (WPRS) in each state,[11] which has been implemented since the end of 1994. The WPRS consists of three basic steps:

- early identification of UI claimants who are likely to exhaust their entitlement to benefits; provision of re-employment services to these claimants; and

- collection of information on outcomes in order to check continuing benefit eligibility and to facilitate evaluations.

Profiling is applied at registration to all unemployed persons who are permanently laid off and who are entitled to UI benefits.[12] A statistical model is used to evaluate the probability that a job-seeker will exhaust his/her UI entitlements. Models are estimated separately for all states and sometimes for regions within states and contain five variables: level of education, last job tenure, change in employment, change in previous occupation/industry, and the local unemployment rate. Anti-discrimination legislation does not allow the use of characteristics such as age, gender and ethnic origin as predictors.

The profiling scores are purely model based and are evaluated each week automatically. The local offices then choose among those claimants with the highest score, according to available places in activation measures.[13] Participation in job-assistance programs is then compulsory at the risk of losing benefit entitlement.

The profiling instrument is used in order to minimize benefit expenditure and as a selection device for the attribution of available places in measures to a formally defined group of recipients.

Evaluation of the effectiveness showed that the mean duration of benefit receipt was two weeks longer for those classified at exhaustion risk of above 70 percent as compared to those below. The introduction of the WPRS made the rate of those exhausting their entitlement drop by 4 percent and shortened the average duration of benefit payments by between half a week and four weeks.[14]

Australia: The Job-seeker Screening Instrument (JSI) and the Job-seeker Assessment Instrument (JAI)

In 1994, the Australian government launched the Working Nation initiative, where a preventive strategy was formulated, the Job Compact. The Job Compact basically tries to increase support to the unemployed as the unemployment duration increases and offers a guaranteed job placement after 18 months.[15] For those at high LTU risk, assistance should start as early as possible in the unemployment period. The assistance is provided as active case management with two basic features:

- the Job-seeker Screening Instrument (JSI), a model-based procedure to attribute a risk score of LTU to all newly registered unemployed and identify those at highest risk;

- the Job-seeker Assessment Instrument (JAI) to define appropriate activities and assistance.

The JSI came into operation in October 1994. It was developed from a statistical model[16] where the statistical coefficients had been translated to a point score attached to a set of prediction variables. The predictors are age, educational attainment, Aboriginal and Torres Strait Islander status, birth in a non-English-speaking country, disability, English-speaking ability, and geographical location. Gender, obviously for equal opportunities legislation, is not included as a variable.

Job-seekers with risk scores above a cut-off point are transferred to additional assessment of their assistance needs. The cut-off point can be varied according to available program places. Also, the model-based profiling is complemented by a judgmental one. Placement officers can select job-seekers within the first 12 months of unemployment for further assessment on the basis of factors like poor motivation, low self-esteem, poor numeracy and literacy skills, and substantial time out of the workforce.

In practice, about 5 percent of new registrations in 1995 were classified as high risk, of which about 70 percent through the JSI and 30 percent through judgment.[17] Another 10 percent of entrants were classified as high risk later in their unemployment period by judgment.

Job-seekers at high risk are assessed for their strengths and weaknesses by the JAI. The JAI consists of a questionnaire with sixteen questions regarding employment strengths, personal barriers and the history of failure to obtain employment. The evaluation of the questionnaire originally led to a grouping of clients at risk into four Client Classification Levels (CCL) from CC1 "easy to place" to CC4 "very hard to place," according to the difficulties placement officers faced in bringing people to employment. In December 1996 the CCL was modified to three groups within major reforms of the employment services.[18] Appropriate measures are related to the CCLs. Clients may have to wait for referrals to case management if not enough places are available. However, once offered, participation in case management is a precondition for continued benefit receipt.

The objective of profiling under the JSI and the JAI is early identification for early intervention by case management for job-seekers at highest risk of LTU. It also has a rationing objective to channel the available funds for measures and case management. As funds were limited, waiting times were too long for job-seekers in need, thus counteracting the early intervention objective.

An evaluation in mid-1996 found that by far and large the early identification procedure had identified job-seekers at highest risk, but there was also evidence of misclassification and dead-weight costs associated with identified persons actually not at high risk. The most serious problem was seen in the fact that the number of job-seekers classified at greatest risk by far exceeded the anticipated numbers and the available funds. The JSI originally had been considered as the primary instrument for identification with a target of about 5 percent of new job-seekers to be selected. The wide use of the additional criteria of the JAI through staff judgment had unexpectedly increased the number of people eligible for case management. The effect was that not enough places were available and some people had to wait for weeks and months, so that early intervention was heavily delayed.

Canada: The Service and Outcome Measurement System (SOMS)

Since June 1995, Canada is testing on a pilot basis a Service and Outcome Measurement System[19] in selected locations to refer eligible job-seekers to the best measures in terms of labor market integration and to the most cost-effective ones in terms of saving benefit payments. The SOMS relies on a combination of model-based "characteristics screening" and judgment by counsellors.

The statistical model has been derived from an analysis of all labor market policy interventions that Canadians have received over the past ten years and the effects that these interventions have had on their employment and earnings history, as well as the costs of these interventions to the public budget. The underlying data file has been constructed by merging 20 existing data files ranging from unemployment benefit files and training interventions files to tax records and census data.

The screening model predicts for each job-seeker with given characteristics which services are most likely to bring him/her back to employment, together with information of the cost-effectiveness for public resources. It creates not only a risk score for the job-seeker, but implicitly a profile of characteristics which is matched with that of appropriate measures.

The model yields basic information about the individual's possibilities through different actions. This information is discussed with the client and results in an action plan to be agreed between client and counsellor. The counsellor of the employment services is not obliged to follow the model predictions; his/her judgment on the client's needs/circumstances can influence the final decision. Thus, the SOMS can be regarded as an additional tool for decision-making of counsellors, which brings general performance data of labor market programs to the decision level.

The SOMS is an information system to guide employment service staff in selecting appropriate services in terms of integration and cost-effectiveness. Through its incorporated database, it is an instrument to evaluate the outcome of LM programs. It is different from other profiling instruments presented here, insofar as it does not attribute a single risk score to a set of client's characteristics, but it generates efficiency outcomes of possible services. The outcome of 25 different programs is predicted conditional on the client's characteristics. The outcome primarily considered is weeks of benefit saving; other outcomes are changes in client earnings, probability of employment and changes in weeks of employment.

Evaluation was carried out after the piloting phase and considered promising to extend the implementation. As the system is permanently updated with the new performance data, it adapts to changes in LM conditions.

The United Kingdom: Structured Job Search

Although there is no formal profiling in the United Kingdom, the British view on profiling is outlined here, because a formal time schedule is set up for preventive purposes. Inflow to LTU seems to be particularly low (cf. Table 2.2). The example should clarify that formal profiling may not yield good results in all countries and that alternative preventive strategies have to be considered when the risk of LTU cannot be appropriately predicted.

The United Kingdom does not rely on a formal profiling model,[20] although extensive research on predicting unemployment duration has been carried out and has been evaluated.[21] The predictive power of statistical-based models is considered to be too weak to found LMP on such instruments. Research could not definitely clarify whether re-employment chances decrease with duration (state dependence).

The United Kingdom labor market offers a high number of job openings with a wide range of qualifications and work conditions, so that formal evaluation of chances to take up a job in a specific segment is hardly possible. Instead of modelling a large range of variables to evaluate individual risk, assistance should start with the problems faced by the individual job-seeker.

The policy of structured job search emphasizes that labor market policy should keep all recipients of unemployment benefits—and not just a subgroup of them determined by profiling—in permanent contact with the information available on all vacancies arising in the economy. All registered unemployed have to maintain active search for work, and the benefit system is operated to keep the unemployed under constant pressure to seek work. Job-search assistance and training supports are provided when it has become clear that an individual is facing particular difficulty in finding employment. Through regular twice-weekly "call-ins" and reassessment of individual perspectives after 13 and 26 weeks and after every six months thereafter, the employment services check whether a job-seeker drops out from the labor market or needs special support through programs.

Although there is no formal profiling in the United Kingdom, a formal time schedule has been set up to decide after regular judgment on the need of preventive activities.

Germany: A Model Project of Profiling

In March 2000, the Federal Employment Services started a model project in three regional employment offices to evaluate profiling as an instrument to identify people at high risk and offer them job-search assistance through case management only a few weeks after registration. The project was initiated by three considerations:

- the observation of the Institute for Employment Research that segmentation of unemployment in a fluid segment with high turnover and a segment of LTU with the risk of exclusion became more and more pronounced and that policy should take preventive action; policy recommendations were laid down in the IAB (Federal Employment Institute) Agenda 1998;

- efforts of the placement service to reorganize work flows in a way to spend more capacities to those unemployed needing assistance with the necessity of identifying this group of unemployed;

- the obligation of the EU *Employment Guidelines* adopted in the German National Action Plans and in the business objectives of the Federal Employment Services to prevent the inflow into LTU.

The project is partly financed through funds of the EU Commission program to modernize public employment services,[22] and it has three objectives:

- to test the power of a statistical model which predicts LTU risk and evaluate its reliability;

- to test the power of judgment-based prediction of risk by placement officers and evaluate its reliability;

- to use both instruments for a random selection of new high-risk job-seekers for individual case management (CM) and find out if CM has a significant impact in the prevention of LTU.

Profiling is carried out for all new entrants between 25 and 55 years of age. New entrants are defined as people who had not been registered during the past six months and did not participate in policy measures during this time. Young people are excluded, because an early prevention program (JUMP 2000) is currently available for this group. Elderly unemployed are excluded to avoid problems with transitory unemployment to retirement. The restriction to *new* entrants is imposed because recent clients often have benefited from in-depth assessment and training where CM possibly would not contribute new aspects. Furthermore, people with obvious health problems and needing medical examination or rehabilitation are also left aside.

The target group for profiling seems to be composed of people with at least some employability prospects. Most come from jobs where they have been made redundant by their employers or from a fixed-term contract which came to an end. Entrants to the labor market from professional education and re-entrants to the labor force are included.

During the experiment, the procedure is as follows: each new entrant is invited for an intake interview. During the interview, the placement officer discusses the labor market prospects of the client and takes notes for the usual placement activities on qualification, job experience and area of job search. Statistical characteristics of the occupation, qualification level, work experience/LM (re-)entrant, sex, age, reason for job loss, immigration and health problems are completed on the profiling form. Together with the regional unemployment rate, these data form the input to the statistical model that produces a group-specific LTU probability.

Placement officers then complete the form with their judgment on several items of the client's deficiencies affecting his/her job perspectives. The judgment is given for items of qualification, mobility, motivation and general deficiencies and classified by no/low/medium/ high risk of LTU, according to the staff's experience. The answers are taken as the input to a judgment-based decision rule to increase or lower the cut-off point for high LTU risk from the statistical model.

The profiling forms are sent to the IAB where the statistical model and the judgment score is formally evaluated according to the decision rules. The rules to generate risk scores and the scores attributed to the unemployed are kept secret during the project time to avoid possible influences on the judgment or behavior of placement officers. The placement officers might increase efforts for the control group in a non-intended competition with CM or neglect activities for persons with a poor score.

The procedure applied in the IAB splits the profiled cases into two groups with low and high LTU risk. The high-risk group again is split by random selection into two groups of equal size. One is the control group that will be treated in the employment offices according to normal rules. The other group will be offered CM as addi-

Table 2.3
Characteristics of Profiling Instruments

	Netherlands	USA	Australia	Canada	Germany
Applied to	new job-seekers	new benefit claimants	new job-seekers	job-seekers	newly unemployed, 25-55 years
Assessment based on	distance to the labour market; probability to find a job	probability to exhaust benefits	probability to become LTU	programme outcome and weeks of benefit savings	probability to become LTU
Timing	early	early	early	early, when needed	early
Classification	reversible	definite	reversible	no	definite for CM selection
Profiling	two-stage	model-based	two-stage	decision tool; no direct profiling	model-and judgement-based
Update of estimation parameters	proposed: yearly	regularly	unknown	permanently through integrated database	ex-post for evaluation
Status	operational	operational	operational	operational in selected offices	experimental
Participation in CM	agreed	compulsory to continue benefit receipt	compulsory to continue benefit receipt	agreed	voluntary
Evaluation	forthcoming: evaluation of Kansmeter handling; proposed: weighting of risk factors	yes	partly	yes	scheduled for end of experiment

tional support in the job search. The profiling stops when 500 unemployed persons complete assessment by CM in each of the employment offices. The project will end in mid-2001 for CM and will be thoroughly evaluated during and after the operational phase.

After one year, the design of the study will allow for the evaluation of the ex-ante prediction of LTU and the effect of CM intervention. By comparison between the low-risk group and the control group, the reliability of the statistical and judgment-based prediction will be checked. It will also allow checking as to whether different weighing of the available variables could improve predictions (ex-post adaptation). A second comparison between the CM group and the control group will show if CM has an effect in preventing LTU.

Participation in CM for the selected group is voluntary. The task of CM will be in-depth assessment of strengths and weaknesses of the client, not only in qualification-related characteristics but also in job-search-related problems like application and self-presentation, motivation and attitudes, mobility or financial problems. CM will propose steps to increase employability, either by adequate measures of the employment offices or by support in resolving individual problems. When needed, CM will accompany job search and working in on the new job. The intention is to offer holistic support to the unemployed right from the start before demotivation by unsuccessful job search or low search efforts can distance the person from the labor market.

The evaluation will tell to what extent the selection in the German labor market works in a predictable or mere hazardous way.

The following table summarizes the characteristics of profiling instruments, as described above.

Conclusions

This survey on profiling reveals that profiling of job-seekers is still a new instrument to formally assist employment services to channel workloads, optimize resources and select appropriate services according to clients' needs or to some efficiency criteria. The different national models vary in their primary objective, the methods used and the degree of complexity.

Profiling instruments help in decision-making as to whom will receive support by LMP and when and what type of support will be offered. The formal approach of these questions through profiling may increase systematic decision-making. Variations in decisions between staff members in need of support may be reduced. Targeting of LMP to those in need can be improved, thus helping to efficiently spend scarce funds.

It remains to be seen if those in need can be correctly identified through these instruments or if identification can at least be improved. Although experience and statistics show that LTU is correlated to the characteristics outlined above, there is still much left to hazard in successful job search. Especially when profiling is used for early identification of LTU risk, the danger of dead loss by misclassification persists. If instruments have the capacity to correctly predict those at highest risk, they will be useful for improving preventive action. Possibly a "structured profiling" with repeated risk assessment at, say, six-month intervals could avoid misclassification. On registration of new job-seekers, only those with highest-risk scores would receive early support. After some time, when the sorting process has worked and an important number of the unemployed have left the register, a second assessment could identify an additional group at less obvious risk. At this stage, job-search experiences from the first phase of unemployment can possibly be evaluated to determine whether it was only misfortune or if there was a specific reason that prevented re-employment.

The impact of profiling instruments may be qualitative as well as quantitative. Assistance in decision-making through a formal check of criteria will certainly improve quality, if the criteria are well defined and objectively determined. There may be a danger that profiling instruments are merely used for rationing scarce resources through cut-off points, where only the highest or lowest scoring have access to jobs or support in LMP. For example, if placement services were to restrict their activities of filling vacancies to job-seekers with low-risk scores, profiling might have a self-fulfilling impact for those at high risk and exclude groups from access to employment. Therefore, a revision of the profiling outcome, if unjustified or outdated, at any stage of the unemployment process seems to be necessary.

Because of the hazards involved in job search, even a good profiling instrument will at least to some extent yield misclassifications. Even among job-seekers generally considered at low LTU risk, some will fail in their job-search efforts and become LTU. Therefore, some funds and resources must be available to support the long-term unemployed, even when a systematic early intervention strategy is followed by employment services.

Generally, the duration of unemployment is measured on a single uninterrupted spell. According to the legislation in specific countries, a spell is interrupted when an unemployed person is considered not to be available for work. This may be the case for periods of participation in training measures or for periods of illness. Also, working on a fixed-term contract for a short period or working unsuccessfully on probation will interrupt a spell and begin a new one. If interruptions occur before 12 months, these spells are formally not accounted for in LTU, although the job-seeker is without stable employment for a longer period.[23] A reduction in the inflow rate to LTU therefore does not necessarily indicate successful prevention if the effect is caused by interruptions only and not by increased exits from employment. Profiling instruments should take into account repeated spells of unemployment or a definition of LTU in a wider sense.[24]

If early intervention against LTU is a prerogative, then rules are needed to determine groups at risk, time of intervention, and type of assistance. Profiling instruments can play a useful role in systematically applying the rules. One has to ask, however, what kind of impact a strategy of early intervention can have. For the individual, early assistance may prevent demotivation and resignation because of unsuccessful job search. It may help to update skills and qualifications to increase employability, and it may lead to earlier re-employment, though no one knows when re-employment would have occurred without intervention. This can only be evaluated in controlled experiments for groups with and without intervention. On the macroeconomic level, early intervention would hardly create more jobs than late or no intervention. It may result in a rearrangement of the queue for labor and open the fast lane for people at high risk, while others at lower risk will have to wait longer. At its best, this would produce a distribution of unemployment duration with less variance and less heterogeneous employment possibilities. This, indeed, would be a significant achievement in the spirit of equal opportunity policies and in the objective to avoid exclusion from earnings and social security.

Notes

1.   OECD (ed.), *Early identification of job-seekers at risk of long-term unemployment. The role of profiling*, OECD Proceedings, 1998.
2.   Before six months of unemployment for young people under 25 years of age.
3.   Regular adaptation to changing conditions would yield a "learning model." An example is given by the Canadian SOMS, see below.
4.   For example, old and young, professionally qualified or not, or with or without health problems.
5.   The inflow rate to LTU is defined as the percentage of an entry cohort that stays for more than 12 months. These rates of 20, 30, and 5 percent respectively are displayed in Figure 2.1 as the intersection of the stayer curve with a 12-month vertical line.
6.   Helmut Rudolph, "Risiko von Langzeitarbeitslosigkeit frühzeitig erkennen," *IAB Werkstattbericht*, no. 14/19.ll.1998.
7.   See Chris Hasluck; Peter Elias; A.E. Green; J. Pitcher, *Identifying people at risk of long-term unemployment: A literature review*, Institute for Employment Research, Warwick, 1997, for a discussion of individual characteristics and LTU in the literature.
8.   SWI, *De Kansmeter* (SWI-Samenwerking Werk & Inkomen), Den Haag; 1998; Jaap De Koning; Peter van Nes, "Prevention in active labour market policy: Is it possible and is it desirable? Lessons from the Dutch experience," *EALE Conference*

Paper, Blankenberge, Netherlands Economic Institute, Rotterdam, Sep. 1998; De Koning, "The chance meter: Measuring the individual chance of long-term unemployment," *Current developments in the evaluation of employment policies*, Conference Paper, Barcelona, 19-20 July 1999, Netherlands Economic Institute, Rotterdam, July 1999a; De Koning, "L'expérience néerlandaise," in *ANPE* 1999, pp. 62-63, 1999b.

9.   In Dutch, the groups are called phases, indicating a sequence of activities for reintegration and emphasizing the dynamic of reversible character of the classification.

10.   De Koning, op. cit, 1999a.

11.   Randall Eberts, "L'expérience américaine," le profilage, in *ANPE* 1999 (Ed.): *Les transformations du marché du travail. Les premiers entretiens de l'emploi.* 30-31/3/1999 Noisy-Le-Grand, pp. 57-61, 1999a; Eberts, "The use of profiling in the United States for early identification and referral of less employable unemployment insurance recipients," in Bernard Gazier (ed), *Employability: Concepts and Policies Report 1998*, Employment Observatory Research Network, IAS Berlin, pp. 121-146, 1999; OECD, op. cit., 1998; Eberts; Christopher O'Leary, "Früherkennung ("Profiling") von Langzeitarbeitslosen und ihre Überweisung" in *Arbeitsmarktmaßnahmen: Erfahrungen und Lehren aus mehreren Ländern*, inforMISEP Nr.60/Winter 1997, S.34-43.

12.   Basic UI benefit entitlement is 26 weeks. LTU therefore has a different meaning in the United States.

13.   The cut-off point for increased risk of exhausting benefits seems to be 70 percent; cf. Eberts, op. cit., 1999a.

14.   Ibid.

15.   Hasluck et al., op. cit., 1997; OECD, op. cit., 1998.

16.   A probit model, estimated on a sample of 17,000 clients who registered in May 1994.

17.   Hasluck et al., op. cit.

18.   OECD, op. cit., 1998, p. 53f.

19.   Ibid.

20.   Bill Wells, L'expérience britannique, in ANPE 1999, pp. 64-73; OECD, op. cit., 1998.

21.   Hasluck et al, op. cit.

22.   Agreement VS/1999/0727.

23.   For Germany, the LTU rate calculated from uninterrupted spells in the unemployment register (1999: 34.6 percent) is lower than the rate from the Labour Force Survey (54.9 percent), which is based on questions to the job-seeker. The individual's period out of employment is obviously longer than the formal recorded spell.

24.   Cumulated duration of unemployment in the last three years, or time without employment since beginning the job search.

3

Two Actors in Employability: The Employer and the Worker

Patrick Bollérot

Introduction

Even though the term employability still does not appear in all the dictionaries and law books, it has become the trend since the early 1990s. Its first applications date back to the turn of the twentieth century, and the concept of employability encompasses several definitions, depending on whether it is used by doctors, statisticians, social workers, the different actors involved in labor market policies, or human resource managers.

In the European Community's terminology, the word employability appeared in the latter half of the 1990s, defined as a capacity to integrate into working life. Since that time, the European Commission has made it a priority of its employment strategy, and a special summit meeting on employment held in Luxembourg in November 1997[1] identified employability as the first of the guidelines for employment starting in 1998.

A complex and constantly changing concept, employability is often used today both as a means of analysis and of understanding the process of selecting job-seekers in the labor market (estimating the probabilities of reintegration on the basis of age, gender, experience, qualification, social handicaps or health condition) and as an element in the internal management of human resources in enterprises (to judge the knowledge required of workers for accomplishing certain tasks and missions connected with their job, employment or trade).

At the juncture of these two concepts, the term employability also serves to define the measure of the competencies acquired or developed by a worker within an enterprise which allow him or her to continue to meet its demands or to apply for employment even outside the enterprise where he or she is presently working.

Indeed, the employability of an individual is the result of a number of positive factors that make up his or her capacity to obtain or to maintain a job. Some of these elements derive from the competencies acquired outside the professional activity (basic training[2] and occupational training) and others stem from the experience and competencies acquired in the enterprise. In fact, employability development, seen as a tool for combating unemployment, may be activated during the job-seeking period (for first-time job-seekers and unemployed workers) and as a preventive measure during the course of professional activity within the enterprise (at the hiring stage, during the execution of the work contract or while under threat of dismissal).

While the concept of employability of the unemployed, whether first-time job-seekers or those seeking a new position, is presently the object of numerous studies and debates, an analysis of the ways to maintain or to develop employability among workers, from the moment they join to their departure from the enterprise, has not produced very copious literature. Thus, the purpose of this chapter is to delve further into the implementation of the concept of employability within the enterprise by defining the role and responsibilities of the protagonists, workers and employers and by describing the content and the reach of the measures that may be applied to that effect.

The acceleration of technical progress and the globalization of the economy have caused a "flexibilization" of organizations and of work, so as to adjust better and more swiftly to market requirements. Under such circumstances, workers must be able to adapt to the perpetually shifting needs of the enterprise.

"What alternative can be offered to the now obsolete promise of a career?" was the question posed by the French employers at its congress on the management of competencies. Since, in all probability, workers will change jobs or even trades several times during their working life, they ought to be constantly concerned in maintaining their employability so as to be reassignable after each career interruption, and their enterprise should offer the means to achieve that aim.

How can the enterprise be endowed with the needed competencies in order to remain competitive in a permanently evolving context, while guaranteeing the workers the possibility of keeping or finding a job? Employers and workers seem to be in the same situation, bound together by employability. Even if the term employability itself encounters difficulties in being adopted by the enterprise, meeting resistance from both sides, it must be admitted that in the corporate environment the idea of employability is recognized in law or in practice.

The Context of Employability in the Enterprise

Responsibility for Promoting Employability

The actors in employability in the enterprise. Implementing the steps and the mechanisms to develop employability calls for different actors in the enterprise: the employer or the workers or their representatives (e.g., works councils, unions).

The employer's role (administration, human resource management and supervision) is of major importance as a factor for providing the means and the information for employability promotion. Indeed, the employer can supply information about the places and the internal or external entities that could provide orientation or counseling about training. The employer can also organize thinking about employability and can offer individual mechanisms for evaluation (self-evaluation, a balance sheet of competencies, regular evaluation sessions) and for occupational progression (making up portfolios of competencies) which improve the worker's awareness of his or her employability. Even though the administration of the enterprise may not have expressly required it, the role of the immediate superiors is vital for promoting continued employability on a daily basis. In permanent contact with the individual worker at each stage of his/her working life, the immediate superior is in the best position to detect any symptoms of possible lack or loss of employability, to draw the attention of the worker to this and to encourage him/her to take on responsibility for building his/her own future.

However, lacking foreknowledge or a personal stake in the developments and needs of the enterprise, unaware of their economic contribution to the enterprise and unwilling to seize the opportunities offered to them, the workers run the risk of being left out and of missing opportunities to maintain and to further develop their employability. The maintenance and development of employability requires an open-mindedness towards change.

In France, for example, the law offers workers with five years' professional experience an opportunity to have their professional abilities recognized as part of the requirements for obtaining a diploma of technological training. Once workers are informed of this possibility, it depends on them to take the necessary steps to grasp this opportunity to obtain a form of validation of their employability.

The workers' representatives also participate in fostering employability in the enterprise, since they play a role in making the workers aware of their interests and of the need to maintain their employability. The workers' representatives are the information messengers (the go-betweens), the agents for change, and the monitors of respect for the workers' rights and the administration's commitments. The social partners thus can serve as a relay to transmit in an intelligible way the information gleaned in consultation with the company works council. They may also reach agreements with the employer (about creating observatories of trades, groupings of companies, job centers, etc.) which will integrate the employability process into the life of the enterprise.

The European school of thought. Who should be responsible for developing employability—the worker or the employer? Traditionally, the European model is split between those who place the responsibility on the worker and the others who feel that it belongs largely to the employer.

In Anglo-Saxon thinking, the responsibility is first and foremost that of the workers themselves, while the employers simply select the most employable workers, those whose profiles correspond most closely to their needs of the moment. This is the understanding of employability that still inspires countries such as the United Kingdom, even though to this day it does not have a standard definition of the term.[3]

In Rhineland capitalism, on the contrary, it is the employer who grants the opportunity for training to the workers in exchange for their loyalty to the company. However, both these theoretical positions have their drawbacks, which are exacerbated these days by the effects of ever-more-rapid technological progress and of economic globalization. In the first model, the business that does not seek to ensure the employability of its personnel may face a lack of qualified staff in certain sectors and positions. The requirement of new skills to meet technological developments and the wait-and-see attitude of employers who do their hiring at the last moment, combined with the effects of economic growth, which tends to reduce the demand for jobs, are creating difficulties in certain professions in finding the necessary qualifications for the firm's development. This situation has been observed not only in areas such as data processing or advanced technology but also in other industries calling for qualified personnel, such as construction and banking. In the second model, due to economic and organizational limitations, the company, despite its own wishes, is no longer able to respect the original social contract guaranteeing job security for its workers. The latter are thus obliged to take their future into their own hands, no longer depending solely on their employer's initiative.

A third European model thus seems to have emerged, linking the worker and the employer with shared responsibility and common interests in a necessary effort to maintain and develop employability.

The worker's responsibility. Whether or not the employer recognizes a social responsibility beyond a strict economic role for providing the worker with the means of maintaining his or her employability, the worker still has a personal responsibility for maintaining this employability. Otherwise, without a will to do so, the worker risks being excluded from the company by no longer fulfilling what is expected of him or her. Later the worker may be forced to join the ranks of the unemployed, isolated on the labor market. In any event, the worker is at least partly the master of his/her destiny.

Everywhere, the responsibility for employability rests on the worker in the first place, and it is generally agreed that the employer's responsibility is limited to the development of the skills necessary for the success of the enterprise. In Finland, for example, there is no obligation as such to maintain employability, albeit many employers who are obliged to dismiss workers provide them with various means of facilitating their in-house reintegration, with the help of their employment services or through appeal to specialized private agencies for training, outplacement, assistance in finding a job, retraining for other companies in the group, etc.

In any case, it is clear that if the employer places excessive responsibility on the workers, it is likely that a structural drift toward unemployability will be created. This is what happens when the shared responsibility of the workers leads to them endorsing projects which depend solely on the immediate needs of the employer. Such is the case when the choice of training programs offered to the workers is based entirely on the search for immediate profits rather than on a long-term plan. In the same way, a laissez-faire managerial strategy may turn out to favor the most competent workers at the expense of those who have a less clear overview of the company and of their own shortfalls in terms of employability.

Some practices could even lead to making the worker responsible for his or her own dismissal for occupational shortcomings in the context of goal-driven management. In some companies, the executives are expected to conduct their own career development. They are supposed to notice, for example, in the group's internal "employment market exchange" which jobs correspond to their profile and apply for them on their own. If a worker is chosen and fails, he or she condemns himself/herself and will find it difficult to get a second chance. If the worker is not accepted in any position, the axe falls and he/she is naturally expected to leave the enterprise of his/her own volition. In both cases, the worker is led to recognize his/her own unemployability and inability to fit into the company and to draw the obvious conclusions.

Tools originally made available to help the workers to evaluate their employability can also lead to opposite results than those intended. Such may be the case with the creation of a record establishing a worker's competencies, aimed in principle to favor labor market mobility from one company to another. This record should allow employers, when hiring, to judge the candidate's aggregate competencies (knowledge of how to behave and how to do the job) and not only those validated by a qualification mark or a diploma. However, the potential arbitrary element and the inclusion of negative remarks, particularly in conflicting situations, may in fact reduce the employability of the worker concerned and hamper his/her efforts at reintegration.

The employer's responsibility. For the French employers' organization, "to make responsible means not only to liberate, to free the initiative, to make the worker a promising actor, but also to give him/her the right to take part in decisions regarding his/her work situation, whatever his/her qualification level may be."

As employers are no longer really prepared to guarantee either full employment or job security, which formerly embodied the normal social contract, could they not at least commit themselves to provide their workers in every case with the best possible means of sustaining and developing their competencies while working in the enterprise as well as in the event of an unavoidable dismissal, so as to preserve their chances of reconverting to employment in another enterprise? The company that could not keep the worker on its staff would at least provide him/her with a sort of "passport" permitting him/her to gain entrance into other enterprises.

Even if the company considers that maintaining the employability of its workers is not a social obligation, it could, nevertheless, be led to favor it in the interest of its own economic success. Furthermore, managing employability gives the company a means to prepare the competencies that will allow it to remain competitive in a changing world and to improve its performance, while indirectly allowing its workers to keep their jobs or to find new ones. For this reason, many employers consider it important to invest in the professional development of their workers, to involve them in the workings and the objectives of the enterprise and to increase their capacity to take initiatives with a view to ensuring the enterprise's long-term growth. "Developing a company's capacity to compete by fostering, among others, the intelligently directed development of the individual's employability, favors innovation and creates greater possibilities for the enterprise. Expanding the enterprise's growth potential also creates employment."[4] However, development of employability will be more apt to create jobs if it is integrated with the development needs of the company's organization and favors its growth.

Employability acquired with only the individual's interests in mind could lead to the worker seeking work in another enterprise where he/she would occupy the position of a worker whose employability is inferior to his/her own (the "waiting line" phenomenon).

Whatever good reasons might persuade the employer to embark on a program of employability, there is no lack of examples of the prejudicial effect of its absence. One instance would be a worker marginalized from any training which would permit him/her to adapt to technological changes; another is that of a worker who is restricted to a very narrow specialization that eventually loses utility in the market. "How can one ignore that the low employability of certain workers who are rejected by the larger enterprises during their reorganization, after 30 years of good and loyal service, is the inevitable outcome of a long-term policy of neglect?"[5]

Many companies believe that their competitiveness is based first and foremost on a massive reduction of their costs. Now, the maintenance of employability requires a significant financial effort, while the reduction of personnel brings immediate savings. Is it not true that the Stock Exchange often welcomes the announcement of massive reorganizations by rocketing indexes? However, the staff cutbacks alone cannot be an effective strategy; it has been shown that enterprises that center their search for competitiveness on the development of competencies enjoy greater growth than those that try to improve their performance purely through savings.

Some cases, albeit marginal ones, have been reported in high-growth sectors such as data processing or advanced technology in which the employers balk at improving the employability of their most qualified workers, in particular by means of regular training courses, for fear that they may put this knowledge to work for their competitors.

Employability: A Concept Still Seldom Used in the Enterprise

The term employability has entered the business language but is often reserved for informal debates, on the fringe of official documents and agreements reached between the social partners. In fact, if "the word dog has never been known to bite," the term employability, while arousing genuine interest, continues to engender a certain degree of distrust, both from employers and from workers or their representatives.

The workers' fears. While admitting their interest in having their competencies recognized and in being granted a chance to develop them, workers fear, at the outset, that the introduction of the idea of employability serves firstly to establish the priorities for dismissal, as the term implies the concept of non-employability. If some workers succeed in cultivating their employability, what will happen to those who cannot or do not wish to follow their example? Employability is thus seen as a factor for potential exclusion. Secondly, the workers worry about the risks of arbitrary judgments and the lack of objective criteria in the employer's evaluation of the employability of one or the other. In truth, the employability concept would rely more on personal qualities than on knowledge and know-how, thus offering fewer guarantees of objectivity.

In the last analysis, the employability of a worker would only be proven by his/her actual appointment to a post that corresponds to his/her employability. As long as the job is not offered, the employability is not ratified. For its strongest opponents, the judgment on an individual's employability during the course of a work contract would be at least useless and would serve, in the worst case, as a means to exert pressure in order to circumvent guarantees provided by collective bargaining.

The workers also worry that they will not all be on an equal footing, since some are more able than others—for personal or professional reasons—to discern the possibilities of improving their employability. Similarly, they fear that the employers may be tempted to encourage, in priority, the development of employability amongst the workers who are most able to undertake a personal investment. In other words, the employability of an individual could be pegged to his/her intrinsic capacity to develop his/her employability.

Employers refer to the idea of competencies. Among those firms that admit a social responsibility in the area of employment, few come out openly in favor of the concept of employability. Even among those that do, some see it as a means of improving their image with public opinion and public authorities by registering a pretended interest in fostering employment. Others only use the concept to shift the responsibility back to the worker for adjusting to the flexibility requirements of the company, or failing to do so. On the other hand, some companies, without actually using the term, have adopted the practice of employability.

Even though the term employability is being used increasingly by employers in practice, companies usually prefer the term competencies, meaning the professional skills needed to occupy a post. Competencies are understood as the aggregate of individual behaviors (know-how and know how to behave) that the worker exhibits in his/her professional activity. The employability of workers is considered, in this case, as the potential realization in the labor market of competencies developed in the enterprise: thus, employability becomes a by-product of competencies. The loss of employability in the labor market, leading to unemployment and marginalization, would be preceded by the loss of competencies in the company. On the other hand, the maintenance of competencies within the enterprise would guarantee the worker's independence, i.e., his/her negotiating power, in the company and on the labor market.

The respective roles of the employer and the worker in the process of constructing competencies are thus distributed in the following way: the worker is co-responsible for acquiring and maintaining his/her competencies, and the employer is in charge of developing the worker's capacities and validating them. The enterprise will have the task of spotting and managing these skills and of maintaining, in collaboration with the workers, each one's capital of competencies. The social partners will be responsible for the qualifications ratified by a professional diploma. According to this system, the coordination required between competencies and qualifications would be negotiated with the employer. Competencies evaluated according to the needs of the enterprise will be more closely linked to the practical realities than would be the case with a static recognition based on a diploma granted by the national system of education through basic training or occupational training outside the enterprise.

In fact, it is this convergence of the objective interests of the employer and the worker around the concept of competencies that will improve the enterprise's performance and develop de facto the employability of the workers. However, since employability goes beyond the boundaries of the enterprise, affecting the worker's capacity to find a job, it exceeds the direct responsibility of employers. On the other hand, since the competencies can only be observed in the workplace, they do come under the latter's responsibility. In other words, employability depends in the long term not on the enterprise but on the condition of the labor market, and in periods of full employment most workers are employable.

The example is often cited of women during the First World War who were suddenly transformed from unemployable to employable by the sheer fact that they were the only persons available when the men were sent to the front. Inversely, in a context of massive unemployment, employability is not equal to employment but simply recognition of a favorable position in a restricted labor market. For that matter, some people think that "the term employability appears when the principle of full employment itself as a socioeconomic optimum is brought into question."[6]

It will be observed that this definition of competencies leads to the devaluation of know-how, traditionally based on the corresponding qualifications and classifications set by collective agreements, to the benefit of knowing how to behave, which can be revealed only in the enterprise. This trend toward individualization is evidently in tune with the flexibility sought by enterprises and leads to a personalization of contractual relations which could, if left unchecked, endanger the status of the worker within the company.

In fact, it is apparent that the idea of making a contract outside the framework of the collective has been spreading since the early 1990s and especially that a shift from payment for a job held to payment for competencies is under way.

Models for promoting employability. Amongst the companies that pursue an employability policy, three models are followed.

The *first* model is applied by those companies that "choose" to build the company of tomorrow with the workers of today, because they operate in a sector in which job security is guaranteed in practice or by law. These are usually public or semi-public companies in industries where competition is at best rather weak. Either their legal status or their socially progressive image commit them to promoting internal career development in order to maintain their standards and the quality of their services or performances. In such enterprises, promoting employability is equal to matching jobs to workers and to managing internal mobility. Maintaining and developing skills requires timely planning of training and retraining of those workers whose jobs are doomed to disappear or to change. This is, in fact, tantamount to predicting which jobs will emerge and which will disappear; it implies assessing existing skills and those to be invented, planning the training as required, and setting up more efficient organization patterns.

The *second* model includes companies with very high turnover rates, due to their exposure to sharp market fluctuations. The firms that have been unable or unwilling to predict such variations either provide their staff with support or allow them access to external retraining. In such cases, the staff member bears the brunt of the responsibility for his/her employability. The worker may be granted access to training, given free time and tools to carry out his/her search, information on the labor market, or accompanying measures. The chances are there for the taking; the worker can seize them or not.

The companies that apply the *third* model share the need to be highly reactive in order to respond to the effects of both globalization and technological development. Subject to fierce competition, they need to have constantly evolving design, production, marketing and management methods. The aim for these companies in the long term is to prepare their workers for changes in the organization of work so that they can adapt to the company's requirements. Each individual lies at the heart of the company's concerns, and the worker's career develops within a professional spectrum (horizontal career development). Thus, management no longer focuses on jobs but on people. This approach aims to ensure each worker permanent employability adjustment and in so doing is a means of preventing being made redundant from the company. Workers must be "symbiotically" linked to their working environment, so to speak, and thus fit for survival in a changing "habitat."

An agreement signed in 1990 by an important French industrial group (Usinor-Sacilor) is an example of skills-based management. The basic idea is that career development should not be governed by job vacancies but by skills defined as operational know-how. This required a thorough review of jobs and restructuring professional careers by consolidating different trades into job types, which in turn encompass various posts. The resulting number of job types was considerably reduced, and bridges were established between trades that were previously hermetically sealed off but which rely on essentially similar skills. This is the management method that allowed for the metal workers to convert to new jobs when market forces brought about a restructuring of the industry.

The Legislator's Intervention

Echoing the European Commission, the media, politicians, researchers, and professionals involved in employment and unemployment have all taken to using the term employability. While the term is not yet universally and officially recognized, specifically as it is not legally defined nor part of legal and contractual language, law and case law do, however, refer to various underlying concepts of employability. In general, these are related to hiring conditions, lifelong learning, reintegration and retraining of workers in the light of labor market trends.

Conditions for Hiring and for Dismissal

By setting more or less restrictive conditions on the employer's right to hire and to fire, legislators affect the labor market as they transform the flexibility/employability relationship. As the employability of an individual is ratified on the spot by his/her hiring or dismissal by the employer (some authors call this the worker's "attraction" in the eyes of potential employers), everything that favors the worker's entrance or continuation in the enterprise becomes a factor of employability.

Some states organize their systems of employment and social protection so as to allow the enterprises flexibility, while guaranteeing the broadest possible social protection for workers and job-seekers. Legislation that is too rigid or an insufficient level of social protection works against employment, since the excessive rigidity deters employers from hiring, and the inadequate social protection condemns the workers who are looking for work to isolation and marginalization.

The strictness of standards for protection from individual dismissal (through no fault of the worker) is often measured against three criteria: the firing procedures, the length of notice for the lay-off and the compensation for dismissal, and the definition of abusive firing and the sanctions laid down if such a dismissal is proven. The Netherlands, for example, ranks first for the strictness of its provisions about dismissals: in that country, in fact, all dismissals are submitted to the public employment service. Generally speaking, all the countries of the European Union impose a notice period, but not all their legislations provide indemnities for dismissal: such is the case in Finland, Belgium, the Netherlands, Germany and Sweden. In the latter two countries, in particular, the collective agreements may carry clauses involving indemnities for dismissal. According to some legislations, the payment of indemnities depends on conditions of seniority or age (Austria, Denmark, Ireland, the United Kingdom). These conditions, related to categories of workers whose chances of finding a new job are slim, in fact reinforce their employability in the enterprise.

In the member states of the European Union, the workers' situation in case of economic dismissal tends to be quite similar, under the influence of the Commission. Such is the fact, for example, in cases of "transfer of enterprises, establishments or parts of establishments." Following the European directive of 1977, modified in 1998, which advocates the maintenance of workers' rights and obliges employers who buy out or absorb another company to employ all its personnel, the national jurisdictions adapted their legislation to the decisions of the European Communities' Court of Justice, and those countries that had not yet recognized this obligation have incorporated this guarantee into their own legislation.

Also under the force of a European guideline established in 1975, all of the member states abide by the obligation to inform the public authorities and to consult with the workers' representatives in cases of collective dismissal, even though the implementation of this obligation may diverge noticeably from one country to another, especially as regards the role of the workers' representatives in the final decision.

In matters related to collective dismissal, the fact remains that national legislations are still quite far apart. The minimum level taken into account for applying the specific regulations varies from ten to fifty job cuts. Thus, the provisions stipulate waiting periods before the dismissal notice or supplementary notifications (to the works councils or to the labor market authorities), which apply in addition to those required for individual dismissals, go into effect. In addition, some special provisions such as social plans (see following) and specific indemnities in certain cases complete the regulations in this regard. On this matter, it should be noted that the Nordic countries (Denmark, Finland and Sweden), Ireland and the United Kingdom do not provide such measures, in contrast to the other states of the European Union. On the world scene, the southern countries of Europe (Greece, Italy, Portugal and Spain), as well as France and Germany, are the nations that are the strictest regarding job protection, while Ireland and the United Kingdom are the most lenient.[7]

The level of job protection can be accompanied either by a high level or a low level of social protection. The states of the European Union can be divided into four broad categories:[8]

- states with a low level of job protection and a high level of social protection (e.g., Denmark and Austria);

- states with a high level of job protection and a low level of social protection (e.g., Italy);

- states with low levels of both job protection and social protection (e.g., the United Kingdom and Ireland);

- states with high levels of both job protection and social protection (e.g., Germany, France and the Netherlands).

Nevertheless, it should be specified that the effect of the combination of job protection level/social protection on the employability of workers will also depend on accompanying measures in favor of the integration or reintegration of individuals and on the national employment policies of each state.[9] In states with low job protection, such as the United Kingdom, the law does not oblige employers to help their dismissed workers to find a job. There are, however, provisions made aiming to favor the reintegration of workers who cannot remain in the company. English law does compel the employer to authorize the redundant worker, provided he/she has at least two years of seniority, to be absent for the time needed to seek new employment (interview, travel, trial run, etc.) without loss of salary. This absence should be for a "reasonable" time, although the law does not specify the duration. The employer who denies the worker the opportunity to take such time off, or who refuses to pay him/her during the absence, is liable to the courts, although the fine cannot exceed two-fifths of the worker's weekly salary.

Ongoing Occupational Training

Continued occupational training is the first way of promoting employability. In all countries, enterprises enjoy great flexibility in setting the conditions for access to the training that they finance. They are the principal source of financing for their personnel's training, even if the public authorities and individuals also participate in assuming some of the training costs. In France, employers are expected to devote 1.5 percent of the total salary to training. The legislator establishes a list of the training activities that fall within the scope of continued training provided for by the law. In particular, the law encompasses activities designed to adapt, promote, prevent, preserve, acquire, maintain or perfect knowledge. This package includes skills assessment which allows the workers to take stock of their abilities and aptitudes and to define their career development, either within or outside the company, as well as the means required to achieve their goals, particularly through training.

Training may be provided by the enterprise or by an outside organization, by agreement with the company. Part of the enterprise's contribution to this training takes the form of an "individual training leave," which allows the worker to undergo training in order to "reach a higher level of qualification, change activity or occupation and open his/her cultural and social horizons." In such cases, the employer's approval on the contents of the training is not required, since this opportunity is meant to fulfil the personal ambitions of the worker, whether professional or not. It may be observed that, while this sort of training is not based on the company's needs, it can improve the employability of the worker, who profits from it by broadening his/her field of knowledge and of skills in other areas than those where he/she usually performs.

The employers' financial commitment for training, whether voluntary or imposed by law, is generally substantial. These company expenditures in France are equal to the total spent by the state. More than 80 percent of the total is destined to workers' training, while the remaining 20 percent finances contracts for combined integration and apprenticeships. However, this commitment conceals some inequalities: occupational training benefits more the executives, the holders of indefinite-term contracts, and male workers in general than it does the less-qualified workers, holders of fixed-term contracts and women workers. The workers of major enterprises apply for such training more often than workers in small companies, which sometimes prefer to pay the statutory contribution for ongoing education than to finance the training of their own personnel.

Training for integration and for reintegration of job-seekers is generally taken over directly by the state (basic training, integration aid) or by unemployment insurance (in this case, they are called active measures to complement unemployment compensation and financing for early retirement schemes) even if, in other respects, the employers are often represented in different bipartite bodies responsible for training. Links between the different types of training within and outside the company (basic, ongoing, individual, reintegration training) remain to be created to ensure coherence, continuity and efficiency in developing employability beyond the professional career of each individual. According to certain authors, this global concept of training could be factored into an employability insurance. This would require permanent connections between the various actors, i.e., the employers, the workers, the state and the regions, within modified structures. But such a process would imply expanding the enterprise's social role upstream and downstream from its economic activity.

Spain has also established an obligatory deduction for ongoing occupational training, but in the majority of European Union countries (Austria, Belgium, Denmark, Ireland, the United Kingdom, Sweden, etc.), there is no such legislation obliging employers to finance occupational training, the framework for it frequently being set by collective agreements. In Germany, retraining is carried out at the expense of the enterprise so as to bring the professional qualifications up to date and adapt them to technological and organizational developments. More than 200 collective agreements contain provisions relating to continued occupational training. Their objective can also be to qualify the personnel so as to avoid dismissals or to allow for reintegration outside the company. Eight of the eleven Länder of the former West Germany have adopted laws that authorize four to five days of training, paid by the employer. Eighty percent of German workers are covered by a collective agreement that includes training clauses.

In the Netherlands, where no law compels the employer to finance occupational training, many branch- or enterprise-wide collective agreements include measures in favor of training, along with a minimal obligation not exceeding 1.25 percent of the salary total.

In the European Union, around 60 percent of enterprises with more than ten workers have provisions for continued occupational training.[10] The highest percentages are found in Denmark (86.8 percent), Germany (85.3 percent), the United Kingdom (81.6 percent), Ireland (76.8 percent) and France (62 percent). The lowest rate was registered in Portugal (13.1 percent). The larger enterprises offer more continued occupational training: 98 percent of those that have more than 1,000 workers, against 52 percent of those with ten to 49 workers. In Germany, however, the training rate is nearly the same for the large and small companies, and in Denmark the rate of access to training is even higher in the small and medium-sized companies than in the large ones, thanks to strong support from the public authorities and the social partners. This is particularly the case with the banks and insurance companies, the public utilities such as electricity, gas and water, the finance companies and automobile repair concerns.

On the contrary, continued occupational training is less developed in the traditional sectors such as textiles, mining, transport, construction, etc. The greatest numbers of workers involved in training programs are to be found in Ireland (43 percent), the United Kingdom (39 percent), France (36 percent) and Denmark (34 percent). The countries of southern Europe (Italy, Spain, Greece and Portugal), where training is less well organized, show the lowest number of hours of training per worker. In general, the companies' experiences in matters of training are closely linked to the national labor market particularities and to the educational system. For example, in the United Kingdom, where the educational system includes very little occupational training, the worker is put directly to work and his/her apprenticeship is accomplished on the job. It is also important to note that continued occupational training is less vital to men than to women workers, who are generally less well qualified and whose degree of employability is lower.

Compulsory reintegration in the context of a social plan. In case of collective dismissal, the law generally provides for consultations and negotiations in search of solutions other than dismissal and of the means to attenuate the effects in the form of complementary measures (reintegration aid, financial aid, etc.). These negotiations are carried out with the workers' representatives (works councils, unions) and, in some cases, with labor market authorities, as happens in Italy, to define the selection criteria. Here again, it is a question of setting in motion measures designed to improve the employability of the persons concerned, either in the company or outside it. In the absence of an agreement, the labor authorities, as in Greece, impose their own conditions or, following the example of Spain, refuse to give their approval.

Several countries (Germany, Austria, the Netherlands, France) require the establishment of a social plan in cases of collective dismissal. For the enterprise, the workers' representatives, and occasionally the competent public authorities, this consists of the obligation to reach complementary agreements describing in detail the measures to be taken regarding transfer (internal or external), retraining, and the conditions for payment of the severance indemnity.

In Germany, the works councils are competent to negotiate binding agreements. The provisions in these social plans may include such elements as retraining, rehiring priorities, gradual reduction of working hours, and the right to be reassigned to another job within the company. The law also provides that the granting of state subsidies to enterprises that negotiate a social plan should be decided by taking into account the measures of assistance offered to the dismissed workers. Some provisions aim to protect the categories of workers for whom reintegration would prove most difficult. The law on protection against dismissals obliges the company to bear in mind also the age of the workers in their social plans.

In Austria as in the Netherlands, a social plan that includes solutions for avoiding the dismissals or measures designed to facilitate the reintegration of the dismissed workers (training, financial aid, support for job hunting, etc.) must be drawn up in companies with more than twenty workers.

French legislation specifies that in the context of massive economic redundancies (enterprises with at least fifty workers and dismissals of at least ten in a period of 30 days) the employer must put a social plan into force to avoid the dismissals or to limit their number and to facilitate the reintegration of the personnel whose dismissal has proved unavoidable. The law of 27 January 1993 stipulates that social plans should contain a specific chapter entitled Reintegration Plan, including in particular the reintegration steps to be taken within or outside the company.

According to the regulations, the duty of seeking all possible reintegration within the enterprise exists even before the dismissal: "The economic redundancy of a worker can only occur if his/her reintegration within the company is impossible" (ruling of the Supreme Court of Appeals, 1 April 1992). "In the event a job needs to be eliminated or modified," the employer must "offer other available jobs in the same category or, should such not be available, in a lower category of employment, to the workers involved, even if this requires a substantial change in their work contract" (ruling of the Supreme Court of Appeals, 8 April 1992). The obligation to retrain should be incorporated into the broader obligation to increase the workers' adaptability, fostering their mobility toward other duties whenever their present position is endangered. Opportunities should be sought in the plant where the post has been eliminated, elsewhere in the enterprise or within the group to which the employer belongs, including among their foreign connections. The courts consider that, in this case, the employer is obliged to obtain results.

The obligation to reintegrate has been extended to cover all economic redundancies without any minimum thresholds. If it is impossible to reintegrate a worker within the enterprise or the group, the employer must make every effort to favor external reintegration and declare in what way he/she plans to assist the worker in finding a new job. This is called the obligation of means.

In other respects, and beyond situations that call for setting in motion a social plan, the enterprise should provide the worker with the means to build up his/her employability by fostering its inherent components. The employer has "the duty to ensure his/her workers' adjustment to changes in their jobs" (Supreme Social Court of Appeal of 25 February 1992).

Having established the employer's obligation to maintain the worker's employability within the company, is there a corresponding obligation on the part of the workers to sustain their employability? It is generally thought that workers have a duty to maintain a certain level of skills. The employer has the right to dismiss a worker for incompetence, unfitness or professional inadequacy. French legislation deems that a worker can only refuse training if this would amount to modifying his/her work contract. The worker must accept training in new techniques, with new tools, and in new work procedures that have been introduced to accomplish his/her job. This obligation, linked to the needs of the company, is a reflection of the employer's responsibility for the worker's adaptation. So far, the obligation to maintain these skills has not extended to sustaining external employability, i.e., the capacity to find a job other than the one presently occupied, which pertains to the interest and responsibility of the individual worker.

Although employability as such is recognized neither by law nor by legislation, at least its constituent elements are. The enterprise, thus, bears responsibility to mobilize its forces, making available the necessary funds and seizing the opportunities that arise to develop its workers' employability.

Implementation of Employability Promotion

Key Opportunities for Employability Promotion

Today, most of the actions undertaken to maintain and develop employability (reintegration units, retraining, skills evaluation, etc.) are part of a social plan, i.e., a corrective stopgap measure after the fact rather than an anticipatory action before a problem arises. Now, in order to fulfil its regulatory role, employability should be built in over the whole career, even for those workers who do not appear to be at risk. In this regard, there are key opportunities for action which avoid operating in emergency situations—an obvious recipe for failure. The employer thus chooses to apply preventive measures so as to maintain the employability of his/her workers, especially the older ones.

The time of hiring and the transitional periods in the worker's life. The time of hiring is the employer's first opportunity to confirm the actual or potential employability of the applicant. By this action, the employer considers that the worker is immediately employable. Most companies, at this juncture, look for knowledge ratified by a diploma (university or professional) rather than aptitudes (linked particularly to the behavior of the individual). As sole judge of the person's capacities at the time of hiring, the employer obviously makes a selection and will usually reject candidates belonging to categories whose employability is less evident at first sight, such as the older unemployed, the long-term unemployed, young unskilled workers, etc. However, the employer's decision may be influenced by external factors, for instance, the possibility of obtaining public subsidies for certain categories of job-seekers or the desire to enhance the company's social image.

Some outside actors, public or private, can also help the employer in the search. Thus, Peugeot sought help from the French employment service (ANPE) to make a hiring preselection for a plant that exports cars exclusively to Japan. Peugeot's instructions were to exclude from this selection women, young workers, people over 47 years of age and the long-term unemployed. The ANPE then asked what degree of "skills" Peugeot required of its future workers. The criteria stipulated were the ability to work in a team, to work under pressure and to work according to strict standards. The ANPE managed to convince the company to alter its selection criteria and finally convinced it to hire 13 percent women, 11 percent workers over 47 years of age, 41 percent young workers and 29 percent long-term unemployed.

Hiring also constitutes a decisive moment for projecting the future. Some workers with low employability may be hired anyway, because the employer calculates that by giving the workers complementary training or by putting their competencies to work on the job their degree of employability will soon be satisfactory. The more the employer develops a hiring policy based on a long-term perspective, the more importance he/she will attach to the candidate's aptitudes and attitudes as essential factors for his/her adjustment to the company. It is advisable to project the middle-term evolution of the worker so as to build up his/her employability over time, thus avoiding later failures.

After hiring, there are two more key occasions to stimulate the worker's employability and anticipate possible stumbling blocks. The end of the trial period, which marks the close of the hiring process, offers an opportunity to re-examine the evolution forecast for the worker, based on the lessons learned from the first months of collaboration. Likewise, throughout a career, the transition periods (two years after beginning work for the young diploma holders; half-way through the career, around the age of 40; and on the threshold of the career's end, near 50 years of age) are also propitious stages for re-examining the individual's situation, taking into account the experience acquired, the capacities, the motivations and the projects of each one. Especially at these key moments, the worker should ask himself/herself about the date of his/her last training, the evaluation of his/her work by superiors, the "transferability" of his/her competencies, his/her unfulfilled potentials, etc., and the enterprise should offer the worker the means to make this self-evaluation and should inform him/her of its future needs regarding competencies and new professions.

Maintenance of employability of older workers. With an ageing workforce, the enterprise must make continual progress in matters of competitiveness and productivity. During the next twenty years, the number of European citizens aged 20 to 29 will diminish by 20 percent. The number of workers between 50 and 64 years of age will increase by 25 percent, and the number of those aged 65 and over will equally increase by 25 percent.[11]

Therefore, the enterprise must learn to foster the employability of the oldest workers. This is particularly important since early retirement provisions, extensively used during the 1980s-1990s as an answer to restructuring and recession problems, seem to have lost ground, due to their high costs and their lack of effect in creating jobs.

Also, in the interests of the retirement systems' financial equilibrium, the trend will rather be to prolong the workers' working life than to reduce the retirement age. "Employers have to formulate innovative employment strategies in order to face an entirely different labor market environment from that of the past."[12] The development of the enterprise with its older workers is not only the result of demographic changes or of the attempt to balance the finances of the retirement systems, but also stems from an element of competitiveness and performance. The European Common Report on Employment, adopted in 1999 by the European Commission, emphasizes the need to "retrain" the older workers and to improve their competencies so as to increase their employability, thereby avoiding the scarcity of qualified workers attributed to the ageing of the workforce. The early retirement of the older workers may entail a loss of know-how and experience to the detriment of the enterprise's competitiveness. Thus, even though the examples may be rare, some companies are beginning to argue in favor of employing older workers: expansion and optimization of the recruitment potential, prevention of scarcity of skilled workers, satisfaction of an older clientele better understood by workers of their generation, a balanced workforce combining youth and maturity, occupational stability, efficiency and cost average equivalent to that of workers from other age brackets.[13]

While employing older workers fulfils the needs of the enterprise, it should nevertheless be accompanied by special measures to maintain their employability so as to, at the same time, incite them to extend their professional life and offer them ways to participate in improving the company's performance. The integrated management of older workers would include the prevention of problems linked with ageing and corrective measures to compensate for a lower level of performance due to ageing, particularly through training at all stages of their careers, as well as policies designed to adapt work stations, schedules and the work environment. As an example, one could cite the Danish company DLG, which employs 2,000 persons and was having difficulty in finding enough qualified staff: most of its workers took early retirement at the age of 60 (the retirement age being 65) and increasingly fewer qualified young people were seeking work. DLG therefore established a "policy for ageing workers" enabling them to continue working after 60 according to arrangements convenient to the individuals and to the company:

- from 55 years of age, a yearly interview to prepare for retirement, during which an adjustment of the work contract can be negotiated;

- from 58 years, an interview with an external adviser, financed by the employer, to discuss the choice between retirement or employment;

- three months before the 60th birthday, signature of an "agreement for the older worker," to establish the worker's intention and the conditions for continuing his/her activity within the company;

- the proposal of a "job for the ageing worker" which may be accompanied by a training course and might involve new tasks, a change, a reduced schedule, etc. Generally speaking, the company continues to pay the employer's part of the retirement contributions on the basis of the preceding salary, but the worker's salary is recalculated in accordance with his/her new schedule and the duties of the new job.

Levers of Employability Promotion

The employer has various levers that can be used in order to set in motion the enterprise's drive to develop the employability of its personnel. These levers may act upon the worker or the company itself. The factors of worker employability depend on the worker's experience and skills, willingness to embark on a preventive course, margin of autonomy, and the breadth of his/her vision in orienting the choices. In order to maintain its workers' employability, the company can expand its communications about its projects and needs in terms of jobs, orient its work organization so as to recognize competencies, encourage training, implementation and recognition of an acquired skill, take part in career management and encourage internal and external mobility. An enterprise that embarks on an employability policy establishes previously the vehicles of employability and the targets for action.

Targets for action. The first targets for action are linked mainly to the worker as a person.[14] It may be a question of inadequacies of basic training or acquired in the context of continued training, an absence of mobility and an open mind toward the outside world, the obsolescence of skills, the lack of reference points to place himself/herself in the performance picture and the absence of cross-competencies, the lack of professional relations, insufficiently diversified professional experience, etc.

Other negative factors are more directly linked to the company. They can be due particularly to a system of classification and remuneration unconnected to the market, to a lack of anticipation in recruitment, to an absence of communication about strategy, a policy on mobility, follow-up on the individuals' careers, a strategic training policy, to a work organization not oriented toward developing skills, to a general lack of vision about the skills needed in the medium term, etc.

Lastly, some targets for action relate more closely to the market as, for example, the opacity of the economic context, the failure to anticipate changes, the rigidity of contractual forms, a faulty management of available resources, etc.

As part of the company's development plan, taking into account all these elements as objects for improvement determines its capacity to meet the challenge of maintaining the employability of its personnel and of achieving its own economic success.

Building a clear vision of the expected level of employability. In every case, the development of the workers' employability must be based on a clearly established view of their personal development needs and of the development prospects of the enterprise and its environment.

For the worker, the knowledge of his/her aptitudes is the first element in the picture. The initiative for the majority of skill evaluation procedures rests most frequently with the employer, albeit it requires a voluntary investment of time and effort on the part of the individual. Apart from the assessment of competencies, which in France pertains to the implementation of legal provisions regarding occupational training, enterprises have developed different evaluation tools: assessments of occupational orientation, portfolios of competencies that indicate what the worker knows and what he/she can do, the skills referentials indicating the gap between the requirements of a post, a job or a trade and the actual skills of the worker at a given moment.

Assessments made with the aid of these tools are a form of confirmation of the worker's competencies within the enterprise, but do not certify his/her employability on the external market. However, it is possible to establish the link between the two. The Vivendi Group, for example, has called upon the public agency for professional training in France (AFPA) as the outside "auditor" of its least-qualified workers. According to their agreement, the AFPA, as the expert, evaluates the professional knowledge of these workers and assumes responsibility for seeing that they take individual training courses to obtain a national diploma, which gives them the option, if necessary, of negotiating this within the company or outside it.

The worker who knows his/her level of skills should be sufficiently aware of job developments, within or outside the company, to take steps to improve his/her employability. Even though the company no longer offers guaranteed careers, it can offer the workers some indications of its strategy and the stakes at play, on the trades it will require in future, on the possibilities of mobility and of access to training. The worker should be capable of understanding the organizational and economic situation in which he/she is working, so as to place himself/herself and develop within it. In order to do this, the enterprise can establish advisory structures for formulating career projects, grant credits for hours of adaptation to carry out these projects, organize employment exchanges or bipartite observation posts on the evolution of jobs and trades, provide information on the bridges linking trades (transversality), and set up a qualifying organization for workers to confirm and gain recognition for their competencies.

Internal and external visibility are not treated in the same way by enterprises. While it is frequently possible to find clear visibility as to the internal market of the company, the worker is rarely provided the means of knowing the external market. However, possibilities do exist, particularly among the major enterprises and their suppliers or subcontractors (represented by small and medium-sized companies), for them to help the latter to develop the employability of their workers. Thus, Renault has set up a training program, recognized by the National Education Department, encompassing the cross-competencies applicable to the trade of operator in the automotive, plastics, glass, and agri-food industries present in the Renault areas of operation. Therefore, in case the enterprise is not able to hire all the young workers that it trains, it guarantees them a common set of competencies that may be used in different companies in its area. Similarly, the Employers' Groups for Integration and Qualification (GEIQ) in France organize career paths for less-qualified workers in order to establish a pool of competencies for a given employment area.

The Vivendi Group has set itself the goal of hiring two-thirds of the young workers whom it takes on under rotation contracts (external training/on-the-job training) and of favoring the reintegration of the remaining one-third in companies that work for the group.

Peugeot has signed 16-month contracts with a temporary employment agency (ADIA) to teach young people under 25 years of age the most complex trades in automobile manufacturing that require long months of apprenticeship. The first four months of training, paid by the regional council, are aimed at getting the young problem workers into a working environment. At the end of their training, they receive a qualification certificate, recognized by the trade, which enables them to apply for a job immediately at any location within the group.

For the manufacturer, the advantage lies in setting up a pool of qualified operators who, in case of shifts in the workload, can be moved to jobs that are impossible to fill through traditional temporary help services. There may be some question about this technique, since these contracts would seem to be incompatible with French law, which stipulates that such interim contracts are reserved for replacement of an absent worker or to a temporary work overload. This stumbling block only highlights the fact that, in certain cases, developing employability may require changes in legislation. Faced with developments in the labor market, the legislator needs to reconcile the worker's protection against job instability with a degree of flexibility in the work contract that can promote the supply of jobs.

Another example is the Belgian Employment Agency, which guarantees to young, unskilled women under 25 years of age, who have difficulty in breaking into the labor market, a ten-month training course to introduce them to the working world and to teach them secretarial skills. At the end of their training, these young women should find an unpaid traineeship in a company. A network for social unity, comprising some 100 companies (including Ahlers, Cockerill Sambre, Glaverbel, Interlabour, Belgian Shell, Société générale de Belgique), the BENSC, which was established in 1998 to combat unemployment and exclusion, offers a traineeship for those who have not found one on their own.

The first object of this traineeship is to modify, with the help of specialized associations, certain attitude problems that constitute an obstacle to employment. The trainee thus continues his/her instruction during a period that varies according to certain set goals. The BENSC hopes to play the role of "enabler" for the reintegration of problem cases.

Measures Fostering Employability at the Three Stages of the Work Contract

The worker's employability is put to the test at the time of hiring, during the course of the work contract and in case of a threat of collective dismissal. At each one of these stages, measures involving the enterprises may be applied, thus increasing the chances of workers' employability meeting the employer's expectations.

Measures designed to enhance employability at the time of hiring. Measures to enhance employability at the time of hiring are generally designed by the public authorities and the unemployment insurance. However, the enterprise is also directly involved, since it is the employer who will ultimately recognize the worker's employability by deciding whether or not to hire him/her for the available job. The company can also be involved in measures established by the public authorities or the unemployment insurance aimed at improving the employability of job-seekers.

Thus, the majority of states of the European Union, in order to combat youth unemployment, have set up specific measures for developing the employability of this category.

In the United Kingdom, the New Deal program, with its objective of improving the qualification level of the least employable youths between 18 and 24 years of age, seeks the collaboration of employers in several areas. Firstly, the whole program is financed by a special tax levied against some thirty former public monopolies that have been privatized. Then, one of the options offered to the youth selected is to be hired by a company for a minimum of six months while being trained on the job. The employer receives a subsidy of about FF[15] 600, plus a contribution to the training of FF 7,500. In case of part-time work, this aid is somewhat reduced. Once the employment service has submitted a list of candidates whose qualifications fit the requirements the employer has stipulated, the employer has total control over the final choice. The employers who participate in the New Deal program sign an agreement with the employment service guaranteeing a training course that leads to a recognized qualification. Unless special circumstances justify otherwise, they are committed to keep on the young worker beyond the six months, not to take advantage of the program to substitute a young worker for a more senior worker, and to guarantee a salary at least as high as the subsidy and, if possible, equal to the normal rate for that post or for an equivalent position. The training may be organized internally or outside the company and should lead to a recognized qualification. This program's purpose is to raise all the participants to a minimum level NVQ2 (the National Vocational Qualifications measures, on five levels, the individual's ability to perform a certain number of tasks, according to recognized criteria in a given professional situation). This system of recognized training gives them a broad scope. The NVQ confirms professional know-how independently from apprenticeships, based on easily transferable standards.

As of June 1998, the New Deal program was extended to include job-seekers who have been unemployed for more than two years. In this case, the employer receives a weekly subsidy of around FF 750 for full-time employment and FF 500 for part-time work; the employer is not compelled to offer special training. For the period 1998-99, 45,000 employers were committed to the New Deal program.

Germany also applies a basic training policy, closely involving the employers in the process of qualification recognition through alternating training. The dual system trains more than two-thirds of one age group. There are recognized apprenticeships in 380 trades. The training takes place either in the company or in occupational training centers. The apprentices are regarded as workers and are entitled to a training remuneration paid by the companies, as stipulated in the collective agreements. The enterprises' participation in occupational training is important, even if interest has dwindled somewhat during recent years. Around one-third of the firms with five to nine workers, half of those with ten to 49 workers, two-thirds with 50 to 499 workers, and nearly all the major enterprises are members of the system. The causes for a slackening of interest may be a lesser demand for apprenticeships, due particularly to the increased policy of cost reduction, to specialization and to professional practices in small companies that do not always correspond to the training, to the absence of trades open to apprenticeships in the new economic sectors, such as the media, to a demand for young workers from other types of vocational training who are better adapted to the enterprises' new expectations, and to a lower than average participation in the new Länder.

In Belgium, the contracts for first work experience and the youth training schemes have been replaced since 1 April 2000 by the First Employment Contract (Convention de premier Emploi or CPE), which is part of the Rosetta Plan. The aim of this contract is to enable every young person to enter the job market within the first six months after leaving school.

The scheme aims to offer young people either a job or a job combined with training or an apprenticeship. To achieve this, the government has declared that any company with over 50 employees on its books must compulsorily have at least 3 percent of young employees under 25 years of age. In addition, the government is encouraging all enterprises, regardless of their size, to employ young persons within the framework of this contract. In return, the companies benefit from a reduction in their social security contributions if they employ young persons who have not completed their higher education course.

The work contract may be full time or part time, fixed term (12 months) or of unlimited duration (in which case only the first 12 months of execution of the contract may be taken into account as a CPE). The young person is entitled to the usual salary for a worker carrying out the same functions.

At the end of the contract, the young person may continue to take advantage of the measures in favor of employment that require proof of a period of unemployment or registration as looking for work (within the employment plan or the occupational transition program).

The measures in favor of employability development among the young or other categories of jobless workers most often open the company's doors only a fraction to them, in the form of a fixed-term contract or a temporary engagement. Now, at the time of hiring, the offer of a fixed-term contract or of a permanent contract places the real employability of the worker within a time frame. In the case of a fixed-term contract, the employability of the candidate is pre-defined, while a permanent contract does not pre-establish a time limit to the employability, recognized by the hiring. National legislations that limit the use of fixed-term contracts by subjecting them to a cause in practice also contribute to employability.

In Finland, fixed-term contracts are limited by the Employment Contract Act only to the replacement of a worker who is sick or is in training, to the on-the-job training periods, to the case of an excessive workload, or for special types of employment like seasonal work. The law in the Netherlands[16] provides that the fixed-term contract is automatically "upgraded" to a permanent contract after the third renewal.

On this point, the European Union adopted on 28 June 1999 a guideline which transposes the framework agreement on fixed-term work that was signed by the European social partners (UNICE-CEEP-CES). By stipulating particularly that employers must inform their workers with fixed-term contracts of posts that are vacant so as to provide them the same opportunity to obtain a permanent post as the other workers, this directive aims to favor the extension of this category of workers' employability.

Similarly, the job stability agreement signed in Spain by the social partners in 1997,[17] aimed to reduce instability in the labor market by changing the distribution between fixed-term jobs and permanent jobs, leads to strengthening employability for the company's workers. This agreement provided two sets of measures. On the one hand are measures to make the permanent contracts more attractive to employers:

- clarification of causes justifying a dismissal for economic reasons;

- reduction of the severance pay for a new type of permanent contract reserved for persons with integration or reintegration problems (e.g., the long-term unemployed, the aged unemployed, the unemployed under 30 years of age, the handicapped);

- during the first two years of the contract, the reduction of the social security contribution by 40 percent when hiring persons who are difficult to integrate or reintegrate. Hiring the over- 45-year-old unemployed for an indefinite time carries with it an additional reduction of 50 percent in the employer's contributions throughout the duration of the contract. Hiring a handicapped worker allows for a reduction of 70 to 90 percent of these contributions, according to the worker's age. It also provides for a 60 percent reduction of these contributions for hiring unemployed women for an indefinite period in professions or activities where they are under-represented;

- tax incentives for hiring these same categories of persons.

On the other hand, this agreement includes measures that limit the use of long-duration fixed-term contracts. This has meant the elimination of temporary contracts aimed to promote employment (12 months) and of special arrangements to foster new undertakings (which usually last about seven months) if they belong to an industry that was not itself limited.

In other respects, rebates in the employer's contributions and tax incentives equivalent to those cited above have been incorporated by law whenever fixed-term contracts are changed into permanent ones, including apprenticeship, training or practice period contracts that reach the legal minimum duration. The overall impact of these measures seems positive, even taking into account the strong growth of the Spanish economy since they went into effect. This may be surmised from the fact that the growth of employment has been keeping pace with the increase in the GDP. The performance shows:

- a significant growth in the number of permanent contracts;

- a decrease in dismissals;

- a considerable number of contract conversions from fixed-term to permanent, particularly for workers who have worked for a long time in the company;

- a lower proportion of fixed-term contracts (they represent about 90 percent of the contracts signed per month), although their number continues to increase;

- a shortening of the average period of fixed-term contracts, due largely to the elimination of long-duration fixed-term contracts.

It is clear that this sort of legislation is designed to truly favor employability, since it augments the "the worker's appeal in the eyes of the employer," particularly by adding financial incentives to hiring the worker. However, it is also to be noted that in this case the increase in the worker's employability is not a result of an improvement in his/her professional competencies. The ambivalence in the term employability permits its use to mean either that an individual has developed personal skills that have led to his/her being hired or that his/her employability has been demonstrated after being hired. Once the worker has been hired, he/she must maintain his/her employability in order to keep the job.

Measures favoring employability while the work contract is in force. The range of tools and procedures for promoting employability is broad: training, aids for mobility, guidance in the professional career, skills evaluation outside the enterprise, assessment of competencies, organized learning, etc. Alongside these "classic" methods, some original provisions have been implemented.

In Portugal, the provision of "alternating employment and training" offers workers the opportunity for continued training during one to 12 months, while allowing the unemployed to acquire experience by replacing the workers during their training programs. This training should be of direct interest to the company and should aim to qualify the worker through training. The Institute for Employment and Occupational Training provides support by paying a share of the substitute's remuneration, up to an equivalent of the minimum legal wage, taking over the employer's contributions and, if required, participating financially in the training of the substitute worker.

Denmark also has leave programs designed to favor job rotation in the labor market. Time off for training is designed for the unemployed as well as for the employed and for the self-employed workers who have held a job during three of the last five years and who could apply for unemployment compensation. During training, a leave of absence allowance is paid, which could reach 100 percent of the maximum unemployment benefit. Workers, unemployed workers and the self-employed may also claim parental leave for consecutive periods that can last from 13 to 52 weeks (per child). The unemployed must fulfil the conditions set for granting unemployment benefits or welfare. During the leave of absence, a benefit is paid equal to 60 percent of the maximum unemployment benefit. A sabbatical leave, for whatever reason, can be granted to workers over 25 years of age for a period that can vary from 13 to 52 weeks. The worker must fulfil the conditions for unemployment insurance and have completed three years of professional activity within the last five years. To fill the vacant post, the employer must hire an unemployed worker who has been registered as unemployed for at least one year. The sabbatical leave allowance paid to the worker is 60 percent of the maximum-rate unemployment benefit.

In Belgium, a different sort of measure obliges the employers at the inter-professional level either to pay a contribution to the Employment Fund, set up by the Federal Ministry of Employment and Labour, amounting to 0.10 percent of the total salary mass and intended to promote employment of the "disadvantaged groups" or to take initiatives by means of a collective labor agreement at the sectoral or enterprise level to promote employment of these "disadvantaged groups." In general, enterprises have preferred to spend these resources on training in the sector, rather than paying them into a fund whose objectives (financing complementary plans) seem more remote. In the collective agreement, the social partners themselves define what they mean by "disadvantaged groups." The nature of these actions is defined by the agreement. They can variously take the form of training initiatives, whether individual or organized by a training center, of job hunting assistance, of help with retraining, etc.

Also in Belgium, the provision for a "career break" is another example of employability promotion in the course of the work contract. Companies have to accept that up to 3 percent of their workers may wish to take a break in their careers. When exceeding the 3 percent threshold, the worker can only interrupt his/her career with the agreement of the employer. In this instance, an unemployed worker replaces the worker who has decided for personal reasons either to take a training course or to stop working. The person who interrupts his/her career receives an allowance to that effect, paid by the unemployment insurance. In 1995, 50,000 persons benefited from this system, which allows the unemployed person to improve his/her employability through a training program and by on-the-job experience and the worker to take time off to receive more training.

Nevertheless, despite the efforts of employer and worker to maintain the latter's employability, it is not always possible to avoid a dismissal, especially for companies facing great economic difficulties.

Measures enhancing employability in cases of collective dismissal. When the employer no longer has any choice but to dismiss part of his/her staff, whether or not the employer has given the workers the means of maintaining their employability at the opportune moment, he/she still can set in motion different mechanisms to facilitate the workers' reintegration. The action the employer takes then constitutes one final promotion of employability, since it aims to ensure its recognition as a new employer.

Thus, the companies belonging to the same group can organize an internal reintegration system for their workers. The job offers of these companies are centralized, training and adjustment measures are programmed, and a hiring priority is granted to the workers of the said group. Internal mobility organized between companies of the same group or in the context of a network of enterprises that share out the jobs among the same workers are models aimed at enhancing labor relations, rather than solving economic problems by firing workers.

In France, the employers' groups (GEs) gather into one association those enterprises whose labor requirements are complementary. The GE recruits the personnel and makes them available to the member companies at times of increased activity or at moments when the companies cannot afford to take on certain competencies by themselves. The workers benefit from stable contracts, but on shared time. Some GEs offer alternating contracts to the unemployed. In certain cases, however, deviations occur when enterprises use the GE for "externalization" operations: an enterprise dismisses some personnel, which it has the GE hire on a fixed-term contract, and the GE then sends them back to the company.

Actions to be taken could also include launching complementary measures to foster the worker's reintegration outside the company. An enterprise that has to make massive cutbacks in personnel sets up an external reintegration unit or calls on an external consulting firm which works out a professional project with the interested parties and supports them through to its completion. This step, which amounts to externalizing the management of redundancies, is generally negotiated with the worker by means of a resignation (outplacement measures). In some cases, the company will help the worker to establish himself/herself independently. For example, Renault makes loans for taking over a Renault auto sales agency to departing workers who seem likely to succeed.

Consequently, what is at stake is to help the worker to find a job as quickly as possible, thus creating an immediate link between the dismissal and internal or external reintegration. Some measures, such as the French conversion agreements, aim to accelerate the reintegration of the worker involved in an economic redundancy in the labor market by offering him/her a personalized assistance to define and carry out his/her reintegration project, the possibility of a training course of up to 300 hours and a guaranteed income during six months. This provision is financed jointly by the state and by the employer's contribution. At the end of the agreement, if the worker is not reclassified, the unemployment insurance system takes over responsibility for him/her. In addition, the worker who has been made redundant for economic reasons or has entered into a conversion agreement during one year from the date of termination of his/her contract enjoys a rehiring priority, if he/she expresses a desire to apply for the said priority within four months of that date. In such a case, the employer must inform the worker of every vacancy that occurs which is compatible with his/her qualifications. Nevertheless, the job must have been submitted previously to a recruitment procedure outside the company, since the employer is not obliged to offer internal vacancies.

In Sweden, "security funds" have been created in order to allow the workers to remain in the company by financing training courses. Also in Sweden, the regional office of the labor market installs a job-searching center in enterprises that announce collective dismissals and connects it to the national data processing system for identification of vacant jobs.

Some collective agreements in Belgium define as "groups at risk" which should benefit as such from specific measures for job promotion as "persons whose job is threatened without complementary training in the sector, independently from their level of education."

Other agreements consider as "groups at risk" persons of at least 50 years of age who are under threat of collective dismissal, a restructuring drive or are confronted with new technologies, as well as workers with low qualifications. At the moment a contract is broken, reintegration measures can also be included in the framework of social plans.

In Germany, in case of bankruptcy or massive dismissals, the employer and the company works council must draw up a plan including measures to avoid the greatest possible number of dismissals, to grant financial compensation to the redundant workers, to propose complementary measures, such as counseling, various types of aid, training, etc. The workers in danger of losing their jobs due to the company's restructuring or its closing can benefit from individual measures needed for their reintegration, such as professional training. The "aid to the social plan mechanism" can substitute these individual supports in a case where compensation for loss of salary has to be paid to more than half of the workers concerned. The employers or the works councils are thus encouraged to assign the resources of the social plans to measures with a positive effect on employment, for example retraining into professions with good job prospects or qualifying measures, rather than to pay severance benefits. This provision can only be implemented if individual job promotion measures would probably be required without it. Subsidies are excluded, since they would principally serve the company's interests and, in particular, be used to qualify workers affected by the closing of one branch of production in order to employ them in another production branch of the same company.

Similarly, aid for the social plan cannot be granted if the workers concerned individually have the option to choose between severance pay and integration measures, even if provisions can be included allowing for some groups of persons to receive severance pay and for others to benefit from integration measures. The maximum amount of this support is calculated by multiplying the number of beneficiaries by the average net amount of unemployment benefits that they could receive if this measure were to apply.

Conclusions

Competencies and employability are twin concepts that are at the same time similar and different. Each aims at increasing the performance of the enterprise while providing the workers the opportunity to maintain and to increase their capital of knowledge so as to not be excluded from the labor market.

However, even though the competencies of a worker are built up and confirmed on the job in an enterprise and cannot be directly or totally transferable to a different context, in the long run the development of employability tends to create favorable conditions for a possible change of professional activity or for being hired by another company. While recognition of competencies finds its first application within the company, confirmation of employability is even more relevant to the labor market. Thus, the criteria for employability are multiple and variable, since they do not only depend on the individual's characteristics (age, gender, qualification, availability, etc.), but also on the socioeconomic context (growth rate, unemployment rate, sectoral or localized crises, etc.).

The object of an employability policy is to adjust the individual's capabilities to changes in the labor market, so that the workers may, at the crucial moment, respond in the best possible way. It is based on the idea that in a company the work relationship is temporary and that the worker should prepare for the possibility that retraining or reintegration may become necessary for him/her.

Some employers discard the policy of employability, either because they believe that the market alone can determine employability and that they have no control over it or, as the scope of employability lies outside the company, it is the exclusive responsibility of the worker. A sizeable number of employers holds that employability is derived from the development of competencies and that the worker who has maintained them has, in their view, a very good chance of keeping his/her job or of finding a new job outside the enterprise. A third category of employers contends that employability pertains to what might be called a "win/win" strategy. The enterprise guarantees the maintenance of the skills in hand and the means to prepare for them to evolve through adequate training programs and an organization adapted to these ends. The worker finds his/her security in responding to the enterprise's demands or prepares for a change of job that does not oblige him/her to start at the bottom (through a training course that leads to a certificate, developing his/her versatility either within the company or turning his/her many skills toward the outside, etc.).

For enterprises, employability promotion is not a case of pure philanthropy, but rather the expression of the will to satisfy well-understood mutual interests. It enables the company to prepare for the future by working on the competencies of its workers, and it satisfies the wishes of the workers by helping them to broaden their knowledge and know-how.

Employability is a game to be played by two, for the stakes are double: the expansion of the skills, by favoring innovation and the performance of the enterprise, contributes to improving competitiveness and, by offering the workers the means to adapt continually to the changes in the labor market, allows them to build continuity in their professional life inside or outside the company's walls.

Thus, it is clear that, according to whether or not their employer accepts to take part in the promotion of employability, the workers find themselves at a disadvantage with regard to the impact of the market on jobs and to the increasing instability of employment. Inequalities also prevail between the workers in enterprises that only apply employability in times of crisis and those workers who work for companies that look ahead and take measures prior to any problems. Finally, inequality is found inside the company. A difference of treatment may exist between workers in the same enterprise, based on their capacities for managing their professional careers, with some forced to accept being hired for only a limited time.

The workers, in this way, remain dependent on the initiative of their employer. This dependence is compounded by the fact that the legislator's role is very limited, with actions not aimed, generally speaking, to favor directly the mechanisms which would guarantee the employability and the mobility of the worker outside the company. In fact, it is mainly in case of a threat of massive dismissals (social plans) or of bankruptcy that some legislations take the objectives of employability into account. In no country does the law compel the employer to maintain the employability of his/her workers during the validity of their work contract.

To counteract the growing number of career interruptions linked to flexibility born of economic competition, as a tool to prevent unemployment and marginalization the generalization of an employability process in the enterprise must be adopted as a social stake in the future. However, the social impact of employability is not restricted to its aim to combat unemployment. It is also felt in the context and the process itself of building employability.

The abilities needed to obtain a job or to find another post are acquired during the whole length of the professional career, within the enterprise or outside it. The state and several social institutions, such as unemployment insurance, participate by financing measures designed to foster the development of just such capacities and act as regulators of the labor market.

Education, occupational training, volunteer work, self-employed work, domestic chores (children's education, aid for parents, etc.) are some of the socially useful forms of work that contribute to build up an individual's "professional status."[18] The reality of this professional status is demonstrated by the existence of social rights that are attached to it and which are, on the one hand, exercised in the enterprise: special leave (educational, training, sabbatical), job alternation, community work projects, savings schemes, part-time work, etc. Applying these rights, that require at the outset a worker's personal decision, will reinforce even more the employability of the beneficiaries if it is part of a career plan.

Enterprises that apply an employability policy have, thus, a special responsibility for encouraging their workers to exercise their social rights to this end and to help them formulate their action plan.

Finally, it remains for the public authorities and the legislator to ensure the coherence of the whole system, so that employability may become the proven instrument of professional continuity.

Notes

1. Presidency Conclusions, Extraordinary European Council Meeting on Employment, 20-21 Nov. 1997.
2. In the European Union, the risks of being out of work vary on average by a ratio of 2 to 1, depending on whether the worker has a diploma of higher education or has just completed his/her formal education (Eurostat).
3. In a 1998 study, the Ministry of National Education and Employment defined employability as "the capacity to develop autonomously within the labour market, so as to realize one's potential in a lasting way, through employment....Employability depends on knowledge, on qualifications and on behaviours that one has, that one uses and that one can present to an employer...."
4. Concetta Lanciaux, Director of Human Resources of the French Group LVMH.
5. Bernard Gazier, Université de Paris 1 and CNRS: "L'employabilité: brève radiographie d'un concept en mutation," in *Sociologie*, 1990.
6. Didier Stephany, "L'employabilité des usages d'un mythe," in *Entreprise et Personnel*, October 1996.
7. See *Perspectives de l'emploi*, OECD, June 1999, p. 49 ff.
8. According to the study by the ILO's *Country Employment Policy Reviews* (CEPRs).
9. See *Perspectives de l'emploi*, OECD, op. cit., p. 49 ff.
10. A survey conducted by Eurostat in 1996 on enterprises with more than ten workers in the first twelve member states.
11. In 1997, the activity rate for workers between 60 and 64 years of age ranged from 10.8 percent in Luxembourg to 54 percent in Sweden (Eurostat).

12.   M. Anders Scharp, President of the Swedish Businessmen's Confederation (SAF), organizer with the European commission of the Conference on Ageing of the European Workforce (Stockholm, September 1999).
13.   When all the costs connected with employment, including the costs of training, are taken into account, "their net average cost varies little according to age." (Prof. A. Walker, Sheffield University, United Kingdom, President of the Observatory of Ageing Persons at the European Commission).
14.   *Développement et emploi*, issue no. 11, 1997.
15.   This is the French franc equivalent to the rate of exchange to the British pound.
16.   Changes in the Civil Code, which went into effect on 1 January 1999.
17.   Law of 26 December 1997
18.   Report by A. Supiot for the European Commission: *Au-delà de l'emploi, transformation du travail et l'avenir du droit du travail*, 1999.

4

Towards a European Model of Employability Insurance? Interaction between Europe and the Member States

Isabelle Chabbert and Nicole Kerschen

Introduction

The idea of employability insurance first emerged at the European community level at a historic moment: the construction of the European social model. In 1997, the Commission of the European Communities launched a debate on the future of social protection in Europe. In a Communication of the Commission of the European Communities,[1] it was recalled that the maintenance of high levels of employment and social protection are among the fundamental objectives of the European community[2] and that social protection constitutes one of the distinctive features of the European social model. It is necessary to modernize and improve social protection so as to make it more effective to employment. The transformation of unemployment insurance into employability insurance was among the proposals put forward by the Commission on this occasion. What would such a transformation imply?

The Commission based its argument on a two-fold observation: the obsolescence of the original unemployment systems, and the lack of convergence between the reforms engaged in certain member states and the state of the labor market. On the one hand, the Commission considered that unemployment systems had originally been devised to provide replacement income to persons temporarily without employment, until such a time as they found employment requiring identical or similar skills. Yet today, given the evolution of the labor market, the unemployed need not only financial assistance, but are also obliged to acquire new skills. On the other hand, the Commission was frankly critical of unemployment insurance reform carried out by certain member states on the grounds of financial constraints. These changes, which tended to lay emphasis on the insurance-based character of unemployment benefit, resulted in a reduction in entitlements for the unemployed, without facilitating their re-entry into the labor market. On the contrary, they resulted in a loss of vocational skills and in social exclusion.

Consequently, the Commission proposed a revision of social protection systems, giving priority to policies which actively enable workers to acquire skills and qualifications likely to favor their entry or re-entry into the labor market, within the framework of a social protection system designed to prevent poverty and social exclusion.

What has become of this proposal since 1997? To what extent has Europe, which does not have a social protection mandate (individual member states are responsible for the organization and financing of their own social protection systems), managed to bring the states to review their individual systems? What role in the process is played by the new coordinated employment strategy?

But this line of questioning also requires an examination of national models of *transformation* from unemployment insurance into employability insurance. What differences are there between existing models? Given these differences, what consensus can be found at the community level? In other words, what are the first elements of a European model of *employability insurance*? This reasoning is based on the *hypothesis* that there is a high degree of interaction between the community level and the national models. Certain models have inspired European thinking. Conversely, European strategy affects and alters national models. Little by little, a European social model is emerging, based on a particular approach to employment and social protection and on the linkages between these two domains.

Europe and Employability Insurance: Where Employment and Social Protection Intersect

At the community level, employability insurance is the fruit of the historic construction of the relation between employment and social protection. It is therefore an integral part of European employment strategy, which has taken form gradually, and of the political project underlying the European social model.

This chapter begins by investigating the manner in which Europe approached the relationship between employment and social protection[3] by a review of several key moments in the construction of social Europe:

- the beginning of the 1990s, with the drawing up of the green book on European social policy,[4] subsequently known as *The Green Book* and the white book on growth, competitiveness, and employment,[5] subsequently known as *The White Book*;

- the crucial year of 1997, with the publication of the Communication of the Commission *Modernizing and improving social protection in the European Union*, the Treaty of Amsterdam and the Luxembourg Jobs Summit.

This will be followed by a detailed analysis of the establishment of employability insurance along the guidelines provided by the coordinated employment strategy.

The Theme of Employability Insurance Emerges at Community Level

A Council Recommendation of July 1992 set out the European method of adapting social protection systems to evolving needs and in particular to the changing labor market.[6] This method is based on the common definition of specific objectives, on the "convergence of policies and objectives." The economic and social integration of all persons fit for work are among these objectives.

From now on, employment and social protection are inseparable. *The White Book* presents social protection as one of the six pillars of national employment systems,[7] and *The Green Book* considers that the themes of employment and the role of the Welfare State are parallel and interrelating.

Subsequently, however, the links between employment and social protection have developed at community level. In less than ten years, we have moved away from a critical approach denouncing the negative affects of social protection on employment towards a more constructive approach calling for a reorientation of social protection to "make it more employment friendly" in the first phase of transformation in view of a "community employment market."[8]

Social protection against employment. Until 1995, the critical approach was very common. Thus, the chapter in *The White Book* entitled, "Transforming growth into employment," argued strongly against three particular aspects of social protection: the fact that it first and foremost benefits those who already have a job and prevents the unemployed from finding work; it is burdensome in terms of compulsory contributions; it removes the incentive to find work. At that time, the views of the Brussels Commission on the subject coincided closely with those of the OECD.[9] Social protection was approached primarily as a financial burden. Thus, the reduction of unemployment benefits is presented as a measure for improving "external flexibility."

However, since then, reservations have been expressed regarding revisions tending to reduce the Welfare State on the grounds that, firstly, too great a reduction in unemployment benefit creates poverty and that, secondly, mechanisms guaranteeing an income must be adapted to operate jointly with active insertion policies. At the same time, social protection is clearly reaffirmed as an essential element of the European social model. *The Green Book* recalls that there is nearly unanimous support among the population for a high level of social protection, a sign of social cohesion and solidarity.

First steps towards action. It therefore became necessary to reconsider the role of the Welfare State. *The Green Book* argues for a new approach between employment and social protection which has today gained widespread popularity. This revolution has adopted the adjective "active." Labor and social protection must be reoriented in such a way as to allow the largest possible number of people to play an active role in society. The aim of social policy is to help people to take themselves in hand and, as far as possible, to play a useful role in society. To this end, more active policies are needed. These first steps lead towards an ambitious political project.

The elaboration of the European method. The White Book puts forward the proposal that the community should develop an overall common strategy based on the transfer of good practice and of experience. The 1994 Essen meeting of the European Council refined this method. The "multilateral monitoring procedure" was established at this meeting, and the five action areas on which national measures for employment should concentrate were defined.[10] The transition from a passive labor market policy to an active policy was also discussed. In this connection, recommendations were made to member states regarding the particular solutions to problems within the five action areas. On the basis of these recommendations, the member states were called on to formulate multi-annual national employment plans. Employment policies implemented are then evaluated, and an annual report on employment records progress achieved in the labor market. This strategy should promote "active subsidiarity." The coordinated employment strategy created by the Treaty of Amsterdam and launched at the Luxembourg Employment Summit is the ultimate outcome of this new method in the field of employment.

Social protection at the service of employment. The European Council meetings in Madrid in December 1995 and in Dublin in December 1996 modified the approach to employment and social protection. The idea of the strengthening of social protection in an active sense first appeared. Thus, the Dublin Declaration on Employment provides that it is essential to:

- ensure "that these systems provide clear incentives for job-seekers to take jobs or participate in other employment-enhancing activities and for employers to hire more workers;

- (develop) social protection systems, so that they not only provide unemployed people with replacement income but also actively encourage participation in or preparation for work, so as better to promote reintegration and reduce dependence."

The term employability is also used in the Dublin Declaration on Employment, where it is linked to groups at risk and to the idea of training.

1997—a decisive turning-point. Three major events led up to this turning point. In March 1997, the Commission established in its Communication that there is a clear and obvious connection between employment and social protection. Social protection systems must be modernized to make them more conducive to employment, within the framework of an active employment policy. To this end, the Commission fixed the following objectives:

- making tax and social benefit systems more employment friendly;

- turning unemployment insurance into an employability insurance;

- rethinking the funding arrangements for social protection;

- implementing flexible mechanisms for managing the transition from work to retirement;

- making social protection promote inclusion.

All these ideas are present in the coordinated employment strategy. The Commission's use of the term employability in its March 1997 Communication on the modernization of social protection appears "not to have been innocent." The use of the concept of employability insurance can be seen as marking the beginning of making unemployment insurance promote employment.

In June 1997, the Treaty of Amsterdam included the promotion of a high level of employment among the Union's objectives (article 2) and introduced a new title on employment into the Treaty on European Union (title VIII, article 125 ff.). The community is responsible, under the coordinated strategy for employment, for producing a qualified, trained and adaptable workforce and for ensuring that labor markets are able to react rapidly to the changing nature of the economy. Emphasis is placed on the employability of the workforce.

In November 1997, some days before the Extraordinary Summit on Employment, which implemented the coordinated strategy for employment earlier than planned, the Presidency of Luxembourg organized a conference on "Modernizing and improving social protection in Europe," in the spirit of the Commission's Communication. In the opening speeches, social protection is considered as contributing to the coordinated employment strategy. The prime minister of Luxembourg[11] referred to it in the following terms:

> "It appears unthinkable to mention employment, its many facets, the challenges and questions which it raises, without placing it within its essential context, that of the future of the European social model, and especially that of social protection....I believe that it is correct to consider unemployment insurance as falling within the larger domain of social protection and security .... We should consider it from the point of view of the need in Europe to move away from essentially passive policies, in respect of employment policies, towards policies which are more and more active."

The linkage also operated in the other direction: "If we do not manage to increase the level of our active populations in Europe, we will encounter the greatest difficulty in financing our social security systems." Social protection is not only working for employment, but employment must also work for social protection. In order to maintain a high level of social protection in Europe, a high level of employment is also necessary.

Integrating unemployment insurance within the coordinated employment strategy. Unemployment insurance was mobilized under the coordinated strategy for employment. This strategy is a weighty and politically cumbersome process. Guidelines for employment are established annually on the basis of the necessary majority. The member states must apply these guidelines within the framework of a national employment plan. The fifteen plans are then evaluated, and recommendations are addressed to the states. The procedure is completed by an annual report on employment.

During the Luxembourg Jobs Summit, employability was taken as the "first pillar" of the European strategy. Employability is defined as "the capacity for people to be employed: it relates not only to the adequacy of their skills but also to incentives and opportunities offered to individuals to seek employment."[12] Thus, the employability insurance set out by the Commission in its Communication of March 1997 has entered the field of employment. But does this mean it has left the field of social protection? It would appear that this is the case, since neither unemployment insurance nor employability insurance figure in the new 1999 Communication of the Commission, which proposes a concerted strategy in respect of social protection, directly inspired by the European strategy for employment.[13]

The Establishment of Employability Insurance on the Basis of Guidelines

Employability insurance has been enriched through contact with employment. The objectives in terms of employability assigned to states via the guidelines have evolved since 1997. Today, four main elements structure the community approach to state action:

- the member states must activate the young and adult unemployed (GL1 and 2);

- the states must move from passive measures to active measures (GL3);

- the states must refocus benefit and tax systems (GL4a);

- the states must establish a prolonged active life policy (GL4b).

These elements partly correspond to the guidelines under the first pillar ("improving employability") of the coordinated employment strategy.

Activate the young and adult unemployed (GL1 and 2). Within a framework of a preventive unemployment strategy, the states should offer a "new start"[14] to two targeted populations: the young and adult unemployed. A slightly different approach is envisaged for each. The young are to be proposed a series of measures (training, retraining, work practice, a job) or "other employability measure," while for unemployed adults, besides these means, vocational guidance may be considered as an adequate measure. These requirements raise the question: What are the "other measures" to be validated by the community institutions?

For the adult unemployed, the member states must seek a balance between preventive and curative measures. What precisely do these concepts involve? In the proposed guidelines for 2000, the Commission supplies a clarification: the "new start" proposed to the young and to the adult unemployed must allow them "effective integration into the labor market." The measure is not simply intended to raise employability, but rather to direct these persons, through their employability, towards an effective integration into the world of work.

Moreover, the Commission involves the social partners in the improvement of employability of the young and adult unemployed, thus supporting a tripartite approach.[15]

Transition from passive to active measures (GL3). The member states must increase the number of persons benefiting from active measures, i.e., training or any similar measure.[16] This guideline concerns the activation of public funds. A target of at least 20 percent is fixed. The guideline is the only one which establishes a quantitative objective. This section underwent a certain amount of alteration, mainly during the drafting of the guidelines for 1999.

At the adoption by the Council in February 1999 of the new guidelines for 1999, GL3 was divided into two parts. A distinction is now made between the active measures, on the one hand (this guideline (GL3), already present in 1998, is unchanged, including the 20 percent objective) and, on the other hand, the refocusing of the benefit and tax systems, which becomes a new guideline. This new guideline is very rich and has two subdivisions.

Refocusing of benefit and tax systems (GL4a). Member states must not only reform their benefit systems to encourage the unemployed to take up work, either through reducing entitlements or instigating harsher sanctions, but also remove obstacles to taking up an activity or a traineeship and make work more financially rewarding. However, these reforms must go beyond unemployment benefit schemes and also have an effect on other social transfer mechanisms, thus covering not only the unemployed, but also the inactive.[17]

This guideline is not in itself concerned with active measures, but is intended to reinforce the active measures contained in guideline

3. It contains another proposal formulated by the Commission in its Communication on social protection of March 1997: "Making tax and social benefit systems more employment friendly" (pt. 2.2.1, p. 6).

Policy for active ageing (GL4b). This guideline marks a real turning point in policy regarding older workers.[18] Its ultimate intention is to suppress pre-retirement or early retirement systems and to promote continued employment by using techniques to activate "older workers."[19] This guideline goes further than the proposals drawn up in the Commission's Communication of March 1997 on social protection regarding the implementation of "flexible systems for managing the transition from work to retirement" (pt. 2.2.4).

In conclusion, it is clear that by becoming part of the coordinated strategy for employment, employability insurance has been given wider scope. The section on "activating people" has been refocused, so as to enable the young and adult unemployed to be effectively integrated into the labor market through raising their employability. There is also an attempt to leave behind the programs which did little more than provide a shuttle service between traineeships and unstable employment. The aims of this section should be achieved through tripartite discussion, involving the social partners in the state's action.

The section on "active measures" has been refined by diversifying its contents to include such active measures as the activation of unemployment funds, the various incentives to return to work, involving unemployment benefit systems and other social benefits, as well as the implementation of a policy to maintain older workers in employment.

National Models of *Transformation* of Unemployment Insurance into Employability Insurance

In this section, it has not been possible to cover all models operating within the fifteen member states of the European Union.[20] The authors chose to concentrate particularly on the Nordic "activating people" model and the British "welfare to work" model, which appear to be alternative models of unemployment insurance transformation in Europe.

For the purposes of this examination, the distinctions used in employment policy by the Nordic researchers have been employed.[21] According to the researchers, "activation policies" are intended, in the short, medium or long term, to return targeted groups, financially dependent on the Welfare State or in danger of being permanently excluded from the job market, to that market by various means (training, traineeships, financial measures, etc.). Activation policies for people are distinct from active employment policies[22] and from activation policies for public expenditure on employment, a broader concept, which includes interventions in job supply by means of subsidies and financial aid to enterprises and, on demand, by training and upgrading the qualifications of job-seekers. In practice, activation policies for people are combined with an approach involving "incentives to take up work" by establishing a link between the level of income guaranteed by social protection and minimum wages. In order to motivate a person to participate in the labor market, the amount and/or the length of period of benefit must be adjusted. However, an activation policy for people may also, depending on the case, be associated with the "workfare" approach, which stipulates a professional activity as a condition to entitlement to social benefits. A system based on workfare puts pressures on individuals and in practice reduces their possible choices.

These different approaches are present to varying degrees and in different combinations in the models analyzed.

The Nordic "Activation of People" Model

The Nordic model is based on a balance, firstly, between the rights and obligations of the individual (the right to a job and the obligation to remain employable) and, secondly, the duty of the public employment service as regards benefits and availability of openings. The Danish model has been chosen as an illustration.

Activation of People and the Right to a Job. In Denmark, a kind of "social contract" has existed since the 1960s, which ensures that every person of working age has a job, allowing him or her to be economically independent and to provide for his or her needs. In the case of loss of job, a voluntary unemployment insurance[23] guarantees a replacement income amounting to 90 percent of the last wage for a maximum period of four years (reduced from seven years in 1994, and from five to four years in 1999). Unemployment benefit is closely linked to the active employment policy.

Since the 1994 labor market reform and its Spring 1995 readjustment, prevention of long-term unemployment and the activation of the unemployed are essential priorities of the Danish policy. Decisions on and implementation of active measures are taken at the local level and take account of the specific conditions of the local labor market. These measures only apply if the unemployed person encounters real difficulties in returning to the labor market, i.e., if his/her unemployment is likely to be prolonged.

The period of benefit is divided into two parts:

- During the first two years of unemployment, the public service is obliged to offer active measures only to unemployed persons who have undergone an evaluation revealing a high likelihood of long-term unemployment. This group must accept the active measures in the form of an "action plan," negotiated between the employment service and the unemployed person, and subject to a formal contract. In cases of disagreement, the decision of last resort lies with the employment service. Other unemployed persons may submit a request to benefit from active measures, but the public service has no obligation towards them.

- Over the next three years, the active measures, which essentially take the form of training, are obligatory for all unemployed workers.

As from the end of 2000, all unemployed persons will have a right and a duty to accept the activation measures before twelve months of unemployment.

It is also the case that since the 1994 reform no active measure can prolong the length of the period of benefit nor give access to new entitlements to unemployment insurance.

Activation of the young and "workfare." Special measures have been established for the young. Until April 1995, all young people of less than 25 years of age could, under certain circumstances, accede to unemployment benefit. Since that date, all young unemployed persons must accept a job or, in the absence of such, training proposed by the public employment service. Those who have not completed an educational cycle are initially offered complementary education lasting at least eighteen months. The income paid to the young throughout the training may be equivalent to a student grant or unemployment benefit. It is the recompense given for the effort they are making to enter the job market.

This closely integrated system provides the unemployed person with a genuine guarantee of resources, as well as the right to profit from active measures aimed at improving his or her employability and return him or her to the labor market under the best possible conditions. However, the employment service retains control over the allotment of the active measures, which must correspond to the needs of the individual. Moreover, considerable pressure is placed on the young unemployed, who receive no remuneration or benefits unless they accept an active measure. This is, therefore, a workfare approach, since the payment of social benefit is made subject to taking action to enter the labor market.

Finally, the Danish government has initiated a major debate under its "Denmark, from here to the year 2000" program, which includes an increase in employment and in the employment rate,[24] a reduction in unemployment[25] and a reduction in the number of persons dependent on social transfers among its objectives.

The debate has dealt with the measures aimed at encouraging employees to remain in active life longer and on the improvement of their status in the employment market. In this connection, the voluntary pre-retirement system financed by unemployment insurance has been modified, rendering access thereto more difficult. The debate also covered real possibilities to reduce the number of persons benefiting from social transfers and the role to be filled by the municipalities in respect of the activation of beneficiaries of aid.

The British "Welfare to Work" Model

In this model, the active measures constitute a *sine qua non* condition for receipt of unemployment benefit. British employability insurance is a two-tier process: firstly, it implements a policy of incentive to work, followed by a policy of activation of the unemployed. The latter policy is merely residual and consists mainly of workfare.

Stage one: Job-seeker allowance. In the first stage, a job-seeker allowance (JSA) is provided, which the British Government considers to be an active measure ("active benefit regime," PAN 1999, p. 6). This is a fixed-rate allowance which falls into two sections: an insurance-based section paid over a period of six months, and a "minimum-income" section paid to persons failing to fulfil the conditions of eligibility to the first section. The latter may claim an allowance for an unlimited period, subject to resources. The job-seeker allowance system therefore covers two types of population.[26] To receive this benefit, job-seekers must prove that they are taking positive steps to search for work.

This measure, focusing on a return to the labor market, includes interventions on the part of the public employment service, providing advice and assistance in seeking a job as well as vocational training for young unemployed persons for the first six months of unemployment and for adult unemployed persons for the first twenty-four months of unemployment.

This support is closely monitored and structured within a tight timetable. The constraints on the job-seekers increase as the period of unemployment lengthens. At the first interview with a personal adviser, the unemployed person signs a "job-seeker agreement," which establishes his/her profile, the types of employment sought, the steps to be taken, and the location of the employment. The rights and obligations of the unemployed person are contained in this contract. If the parties fail to reach agreement on the content of the contract, the situation is resolved by an independent state employee. Job-seekers must visit the job center every fifteen days for an interview. After thirteen weeks of unemployment, job-seekers are obliged to accept a wider range of employment, and at six months the terms of their contract are reduced, in particular with respect to the minimum wage to which they aspire.

The notion of "suitable employment" does not exist in Great Britain: job-seekers must prove that their refusal to accept an offer is for a "good cause."[27] In the absence of a good cause, the allowances are cancelled for a period of twenty-six weeks, which corresponds to the total period of payments.

This model is therefore resolutely turned towards the labor market and provides a strong incentive for the unemployed to take up employment, whatever that employment might be. This characteristic has caused certain authors to describe the British system as "a liberal regime practising a low wage policy."[28] The creation by the government of a financial compensation for taking up a low-paid job would appear to confirm this. The "working families' tax credit," which replaced the "family credit" in October 1999, is a permanent financial aid to low-income families with at least one child. The credit is allocated to whomever of the couple is employed for less than sixteen hours in the week. The introduction by Prime Minister Tony Blair of a "national minimum wage" (PAN 1999, p. 13) does not appear to have changed this situation, except in the case of certain categories of low-qualified women.[29]

This first stage of the British system is based on the idea that the labor market must absorb the flow of job-seekers during the first months of unemployment. Thus, the objective of raising the skills and qualifications of the unemployed is absent from this policy. First and foremost, it is a "back-to-work policy." There are other elements to it, however. Some disadvantaged categories of the population are immediately eligible for the specific measures provided by the New Deal program (see following).

Stage two: The New Deal program. The second stage consists of activating the unemployed through the New Deal program, which aims to bring targeted groups—the young, the long-term unemployed and certain disadvantaged populations—onto the labor market or into any other activity, either directly or through various schemes. This activation only comes into play secondarily and is very restricted in scope.

Basically, the New Deal for Young People applies to persons aged between 18 and 24 years who have been unemployed for at least six months. It begins with an intensive four-month period called the New Deal Gateway, during which the young are monitored by advisers and receive information and vocational training. If, at the end of this period, they are not ready for work or have not found employment, several options are open to them: a subsidized job in the private sector for a period of six months or the possibility of an independent activity, work for a six-month period in an association or in the environment, or full-time training leading to employment for a maximum period of one year. Under the New Deal for Long-Term Unemployed Adults (over 25), those who have been unemployed for more than two years are proposed a subsidized job in the private sector for six months. The unqualified can engage in full-time studies and continue to receive allowances. These programs call for an investment both on the part of the individuals concerned and on the enterprises.[30]

Should the job-seeker refuse to choose one of these options, his/her allowances are suspended for a period of two weeks (or even four weeks for a second refusal). This obligation recalls the workfare approach, which stipulates a professional activity as a prerequisite to entitlement to social benefits. In the British New Deal program, this requirement is wider, covering not only a professional activity but also any other active measure proposed by the employment service. Cash benefits are reduced if the beneficiaries do not wish to accept a job offer or take up training. However, contrary to the first stage, the New Deal does not merely imply a more or less obligatory return to the labor market. Other active measures, such as training or a return to education, are provided for. Consequently, an immediate return to work is not the primary objective. The second stage aims above all at improving the employability of job-seekers.

Extension of the New Deal program to disadvantaged categories. These schemes were extended to inactive populations by the British 1998 Action Plan for Employment. These populations, including such groups as lone parents and disabled persons, had hitherto not been called on to actively seek employment. Specific measures were proposed to them, inspired by the New Deal for Young People and the New Deal for Long-Term Unemployed, to enable them to take up employment or follow training programs. They became immediately eligible for these measures.

The 1999 Action Plan for Employment continued this extension in two directions. Categories previously considered as "disadvantaged" (ex-convicts, persons with low qualifications, former soldiers, victims of mass redundancies) have immediate access, i.e., without a qualifying period and without passing through the first stage, to the existing programs under the New Deal or to specific measures. These categories, containing both unemployed and inactive persons, have been identified as populations at risk, threatened by long-term unemployment and consequently needing special support. The unemployed persons' partners and older workers may also benefit from the active measures, though in their case only after a lapse of six months.

An experimental program has been added to this policy: "single work focused gateway." This is aimed at the entire population of working age. It offers support to individuals, while at the same time exploring with them the different opportunities of a return to work, helping to solve such material problems as looking after children and advising on the allowances available. As from April 2000, persons covered by this system will find their allowances cancelled unless they present themselves at the relevant office. The goal of the program is to make them economically independent. Beyond this, the system involves dividing the public between those who can work and those who are unable to undertake professional activity and between the employable and the rest. This selection process provides a new definition of the populations who have a true need of a social assistance and action policy.

This description shows that British unemployment insurance appears to be a tool used by the state to exert a powerful influence on individual behavior, but with a positive goal: economic independence. It is a liberal, Beveridge-style vision of the labor market, a flexible labor market over which the state cannot exercise direct control. From the beginning of the twentieth century, Beveridge used unemployment benefit as a transformation tool for the British social system, making it possible to separate the unemployed from the indigent and to structure a stable labor market by guaranteeing a social cover to workers in return for contributions linked to a certain behavior on the labor market.[31] Tony Blair's government is part of this very British tradition. The job-seeker allowance and the New Deal are both instruments to transform the labor market and, beyond it, the British social system. "Welfare to work" presents a series of opportunities to people—employment, training or education—which they are obliged to accept. A duty to work or at least to render themselves employable is therefore incumbent on them.

Which model provides the inspiration for social Europe?

First Elements of a European Model

At the end of this demonstration—at the community model and national model level—a European social model can be discerned, the outline of which may still be vague but which possesses certain clear features.

Activation seems to be a key word. Traditionally, unemployment insurance comes into play after the event, proposing a compensation for the loss of employment in the form of an allowance or a replacement income. Employability insurance aims to go beyond compensation by proposing an outcome involving a return to the labor market. It is part of a political project based on participation in active life of the largest possible number of individuals. If the improvement of employability is the employment objective to be attained, the measures to be taken call for a specific approach. This turns around three axes:

- the activation of funds,

- the activation of people,

- the activation of institutions.

The Activation of Funds

There are two different lines of attack regarding the activation of funds. Firstly, the reform of unemployment benefit is a prerequisite to the establishment of a policy to activate the unemployed. The aim is not only to reduce public expenditure, but also to "strengthen economic incentives to work" by making unemployment benefit less favorable. Stricter criteria for eligibility, reductions in the rates of replacement income and more limited periods of payment of benefits are among the measures under consideration. Equally, stricter requirements of availability on the labor market and a hardening of the sanctions in cases of refusal of employment or training will bring pressure to bear on the unemployed. Employment-friendly benefit also involves making the payment of benefits dependent on the efforts undertaken by beneficiaries to enter or re-enter the labor market.

Secondly, the activation of funds includes the transformation of unemployment benefit into financial assistance to active measures—training or any other equivalent measure. Here, more innovative aspects appear. Many states have established national objectives for the reduction of the "dependence rates" of working-age populations in respect of social transfers. With this aim in view, they activate other social benefit funds besides the unemployment benefit fund. Some states allow the unemployed to continue to receive unemployment allowances or any other minimum income, at least partially, after taking up a new activity. This may be a temporary measure designed to compensate for the loss in wages accepted by the unemployed person on resumption of a professional activity—the French regulation concerning "limited activity" (activité réduite) is one of these measures—or it may be an essential part of a work-incentive policy guaranteeing a certain level of income to "poorer workers." The British system's "working families credit" is an example of this. The suspension of pre- or early retirement for older workers and the utilization of the funds normally allocated for that purpose to raising the employability of these same workers is another interesting new feature.[32]

To what extent have combinations of "economic incentives to work" and "financial assistance to active measures" been achieved? The results recorded by the Commission are moderate. Although the improvement of the "incentive-based character of the system...of benefit would appear to be of general concern among member states, major changes in policy are rare,"[33] and there appears to be resistance to reform. Thus, the European Confederation of Trade Unions stated its opposition to the use of activating employment policies as a pretext to calling the right to unemployment benefit into question.[34]

The Activation of People

Employability insurance requires a link between unemployment allowances and active measures. The active measures are considered to be a "new chance" offered to individuals. The term individuals refers to the population of working age, including both the unemployed and certain categories of inactive persons. The new chance is intended to remove them from dependence on social benefits and to bring them into active participation in society. But what do these active measures involve? Some clarification has been made of their aims and contents.

Thus, the 1999 *Joint Report on Employment* specifies that active measures are "aimed at increasing the qualifications of the unemployed" (p.37). This notion goes further than the wording of the guidelines. It is not simply a matter of encouraging a person to take up a professional activity. Training, or any other equivalent measure, must aim at strengthening the unemployed person's ability to re-enter the labor market.

Active measures must be part of preventive and not curative policies. states must identify individual needs in advance. Thus, the measures contained in the British Action Plan for Employment do not fulfil this requirement. According to the 1999 *Joint Report on Employment*, the British system does not provide preventive measures to protect persons exposed to a high likelihood of long-term unemployment. Two features of the system pose a problem: firstly, the measures only take effect after a time lapse after a certain period of unemployment, and, secondly, an individual evaluation of the degree of likelihood involved is lacking. The New Deal program is based on target categories which are defined administratively. Broadly speaking, the community institutions appear to reject an incentive-to-work policy when not associated with a policy of activation of people.

The authors' survey of national action plans for employment reveals that the member states' concepts as to the contents of the active measures differ. This divergence has created problems. The absence of a common definition meant that the community institutions were unable to say whether or not the goal of 20 percent was attained. Equally, they were obliged to clarify the notion of active measures. The 1999 *Joint Report on Employment* states that "these measures cover training, including return into the regular education system or adult training system, as well as similar measures such as subsidized employment, employment plans and assistance granted to the unemployed to create their own employment" (p.37). However, the European institutions excluded programs which were limited to vocational guidance and assistance in seeking a job. Consequently, the United Kingdom is supposed to bring its systems into harmony with the European guidelines.

From the legal point of view, the activation of people involves the recognition of rights: the right to benefits and the right to active measures, and the assigning of duties: the individual's duty to seek employment and the duty to raise his or her employability. For adults, the rights and duties appear to be balanced, while for the young duties seem to outweigh the rights. Rights and obligations are formalized in a contract concluded between the individual and the public employment service. This service also has obligations towards the individual (see following). The contract is the legal instrument which transforms unemployment insurance into employability insurance. The individual becomes an actor in his or her own passage towards employment.

The Activation of Institutions

The implementation of active policies implies both the modernization of the public employment service and the mobilization of all the institutional actors, especially the state and the social partners.

The European employment strategy contributes positively to the current modernization of the employment services by redefining their role in the implementation of preventive and active labor market policies. All their action must be based on an "individualized approach to the unemployed" and on "the prevention of long-term unemployment." To achieve this, new tools must be put into place. According to the 1999 *Joint Report on Employment*, the services proposed in several member states now operate more clearly in "several stages, which begin shortly after registration, with an interview aimed at establishing needs and prospects and at formulating an individual action plan, and continue with more intensive aid to persons likely to slip into long-term unemployment, and by a closer follow-up of progress towards entry or re-entry of the job market"(p.38). This refocusing of the employment services must be accompanied by additional measures.[35]

The coordinated employment strategy obliges states to provide opportunities to individuals. But the states cannot fulfil this obligation alone. The social partners are also called on to participate in the creation of new opportunities. A right to employment can thus be seen emerging at the European level, which is to be guaranteed both by the states and by the social partners. Depending on the countries, this triple relationship takes the form either of "tripartism" or of "partnership."

Conclusions

In conclusion, it can be questioned whether, as the social model develops through the coordinated employment strategy, employability insurance remains a relevant means of progressing towards a society obliged to offer active participation to the largest possible number of people. What risks should be covered by such an insurance: non-employability—a risk considered by some authors to be eminently foreseeable? Moreover, can insurance as a social protection technique still provide real security to individuals and under what conditions? The time appears ripe to weigh up the advantages and disadvantages of employability insurance, the public employment service and the techniques put forward as being the most innovative, such as the "social withdrawing entitlements."[36]

Notes

1. Communication of the Commission of the European Communities of 12 March 1997: *Modernizing and improving social protection in the European Union*, Com (97) 102, final.
2. Article 2 of the Treaty on European Union.
3. Here, the contribution will remain very slight. The authors are currently working on a research project entitled, "Employability as a transformation factor in employment in Europe. Three significant examples: Denmark, the Netherlands and the United Kingdom," financed by the French Ministry of Research. This paper will examine the construction of the European social model from the angle of the fields of employment and social protection.
4. COM (93) 551 DG V.
5. COM (93) 700, December 1993.
6. Council Recommendation of 27 July 1992 regarding the convergence of objectives and social protection policies (92/442/EEC).
7. Alongside education, labor legislation, labor contracts, contractual negotiation systems and enterprise management conditions, p. 17.
8. *The White Book*, p. 158.
9. OECD employment strategy, *Improve the image of work: Taxation, social benefits, employment and unemployment.*

10.   These include the reduction of indirect wage costs, the transition from a passive labor market policy to an active policy, and strengthening measures in support of groups particularly affected by unemployment (the young, women, older workers, long-term unemployed).

11.   Opening speech, Mondorf Colloquium on "Modernizing and improving social protection" (10-2 November 1997), *Bulletin luxembourgeois des questions sociales*, 1997, Vol. 4, p .4.

12.   Commission of the European Communities, *Proposal for guidelines for member States employment policies*, 1998, COM (97) 497/2.

13.   The fate of unemployment insurance is discussed in relation to developments within the public employment services, as clearly demonstrated at the European Seminar organized by the UNEDIC, the body responsible for the management of unemployment insurance in France, on the theme of "Unemployment insurance and employability: What lessons can be drawn from the European experience for the modernization of social protection?" Paris, 23-24 April 1998.

14.   In order to influence the trend in youth and long-term unemployment, the member states will intensify their efforts to develop preventive and employability-oriented strategies, building on the early identification of individual needs. . . .The member states will ensure that every unemployed young person is offered a new start before reaching six months of unemployment, in the form of training, retraining, work practice, a job or other employability measure; unemployed adults are also offered a fresh start before reaching 12 months of unemployment by one of the aforementioned means or, more generally, by accompanying individual vocational guidance (GL1 and 2).

15.   The social partners are urged, at their various levels of responsibility and action, to conclude as soon as possible agreements with a view to increasing the possibilities for training, work experience, traineeships or other measures likely to promote the employability of the young and adult unemployed and to promote their entry into the job market (GL 5, modified).

16.   Each member state will endeavor to increase significantly the number of persons benefiting from active measures....In order to increase the numbers of unemployed who are offered training or any similar measure, it will in particular fix a target, in the light of its starting situation, of gradually achieving the average of the three most successful member states and at least 20 percent (GL 3).

17.   Each member state will review and, where appropriate, refocus its benefit and tax system and provide incentives for unemployed or inactive people to seek and take up work or measures to enhance their employability and for employers to create new jobs (GL4a).

18.   In addition, it is important to develop, in the context of a policy for active ageing, measures such as maintaining working capacity, lifelong learning and other flexible working arrangements, so that older workers are also able to participate actively in working life (GL4b).

19.   Communication of the Commission of 21 May 1999: *Towards a Europe for all ages: Promoting prosperity and solidarity between the generations*, COM (1999) 221 Final. Chairs' discussion document: *The employability of older workers and their situation on the labour market* (Informal Meeting of Ministers, July 1999, Finland).

20.   Due mainly to the authors' progress in respect of research under way in this field.

21.   Jon Anders Dropping; Bjorn Hvinden; Kirsten Vik: "Activation policies in the Nordic countries," in Mikko Kautto (ed.), *Nordic social policy: Changing Welfare States*, Routledge, London and New York, 1999, p. 133.

22. As opposed to a passive employment policy, which gives priority to unemployment benefit.
23. Seventy-five percent of employees are insured against the risk of unemployment; the remaining 25 percent are covered by the national scheme.
24. Creation of 200,000 jobs between 1998 and 2005; increase in the employment rate from 77.8 percent in 1997 to 81 percent in 2005.
25. Five percent reduction in and maintenance of a low level of unemployment.
26. Besides the JSA, there is also "income support," social assistance. Income support is paid to persons over 16 years of age whose income (wages and savings) is very low. These may include single parents, handicapped persons, the chronically sick and the retired. Since 1998, the first two categories have been covered by the New Deal program.
27. The decision as to whether a refusal is for "good cause" is taken by an independent state employee. The latter must take account of the restrictions listed under Regulation 72 of the Job-Seeker Allowance Act of 1995. This list is non-restrictive: whether the proposed job may be harmful to the health of the job-seeker, liable to cause particular physical or mental stress, be contrary to religious convictions or conscientious objections, if the responsibilities of the job-seeker, such as family responsibilities rendering acceptance of the job proposed unreasonable, travelling time or expenses to the job-seeker out of proportion to the proposed wage. Account must also be taken of such other reasons given by the job-seeker in the job-seeker agreement.
28. Yves Chassard: "Assistance sociale et emploi: les leçons de l'expérience britannique," in *Droit social*, 1998, no. 3, p. 269.
29. It was fixed at a low level (£3.60 an hour for workers). The minimum wage for persons aged from 18 to 21 years and for persons enrolled in the training programs was set lower still.
30. Employers participating in the New Deal program must sign a convention with the public employment service by which they guarantee training leading to a recognized qualification. They also undertake, except in the case of particular exonerating circumstances, to maintain the young person in his/her job for more than six months, not to use the program to replace an employee, to guarantee a wage at least equivalent to the subsidy received and, if possible, corresponding to the job or to an equivalent job.
31. William Beveridge, *Unemployment, a problem of industry*, Longmans, Green and Co., London, 1909.
32. Communication of the Commission: "Towards a Europe for all ages," May 1999; Informal Meeting of Ministers of Labour and Social Affairs on "The employability of older workers and their situation in the labour market," held in July 1999 in Finland.
33. *Joint Report on Employment*, 1999, doc. 13607/99, 2 Dec. 1999, p.39.
34. ECTU: First opinion of the ECTU on the Communication of the Commission "Modernizing and improving social protection in the European Union" adopted by the Executive Committee, 6 March 1998.
35. Draft Communication of the Commission: *Modernizing the public employment services to support the coordinated employment strategy.*
36. Robert Salais: "Procurer une sécurité dans une économie flexible," in *Modernisation et amélioration de la protection sociale*, Conférence de Mondort, Nov. 1997; *Bulletin luxembourgeois des questions sociales*, 1994, vol. 4 p.45; Alain Supiot (under the direction of): *Au-delà de l'emploi: Transformations du travail et devenir du droit du travail en Europe,* Flammarion, Paris, 1999, p.90.

Part 2

Dynamic Approaches

5

In Search of Improving Employability

Introduction

In November 1997, the European Commission developed an employment strategy which establishes a common framework for member States' employment policies (employment guidelines), based on commonly defined objectives as well as multilateral mechanisms for monitoring and evaluating progress. It also set up the basis for a wider partnership involving social partners and all local actors. It furthermore called for an integrated, comprehensive and more consistent response organized around four pillars promoting: sustainable employability, a new entrepreneurship culture, adaptability of work organization and human resources, and equal opportunities on the labor market.

In the employment policy guidelines, improving employability is focused on the unemployed or those excluded from the labor market. It calls for a more preventive and active approach towards the unemployed. It refers to measures aiming at improving their working capacity, their willingness to work and their access to the labor market. However, the integrated and comprehensive approach developed in the employment strategy concerns both the demand and the supply sides and means not only increasing skills and human capital but also overcoming a number of obstacles preventing people to access to jobs or to remain in stable jobs and increase their earnings.

The following chapter seeks to look into the operational content of employability and its strategical meaning for the policy debate. The chosen examples are by no means exhaustive, but are intended to focus on different existing approaches and their impact.

The examination and evaluation of efforts and progress made by the member states in improving employability clearly show that in most cases this objective calls for a new focus of their active labor market policy mix and for a new way of delivering services. They also show that the common orientation towards a dynamic and comprehensive notion of employability proceeds at different paces and leaves room for various understandings and uses of employability.

This situation becomes all the more obvious when looking at countries outside the European Union—be they industrialized, in transition or developing countries—which are equally concerned explicitly or implicitly with improving the employability of the jobless by developing policies with a view to tackling the various labor market problems.

The notion of employability is not universally accepted and remains controversial. Employability remains often ill-defined, and common employment concerns leave broad scope for different employability approaches. However, there is no doubt that improving employability calls for a complex and variable policy mix and that employability-oriented policies face various trade-offs and dilemmas whose solutions depend on specific and local contexts, thus raising a major policy issue regarding their extension on a wider scale.

Selected Examples from European Union Countries

The New Deals in the United Kingdom

Nigel Meager

The Labour Government, elected in the United Kingdom in May 1997, has introduced a range of new active labor market policies, the so-called New Deals. The largest of these is the New Deal for Young People (NDYP) aged 18-24, which was piloted in 12 local areas ("pathfinder" areas) in January 1998 before being extended nationwide in April 1998. In addition, there are New Deals for a range of other target groups, notably:

- the New Deal for Long-Term Unemployed (NDLTU) aged 25-plus, which was introduced on a national basis in June 1998 (with further variants of the scheme being piloted from November 1998);

- the New Deal for Lone Parents (piloted in July 1997 and extended in April 1998 and October 1998);

- the New Deal for Disabled People (piloted over the period October 1998-April 2000);

- the New Deal for Older People (aged 50-plus), piloted from October 1999 and to be extended nationwide during 2,000.

It is worth stressing that whereas the New Deals for Young People and Long-Term Unemployed are targeted at unemployed people (more specifically, they are targeted at claimants of the main benefit for unemployed people: Job-seekers' Allowance (JSA)), the New Deals for Lone Parents, Disabled People and Older People are also, to a greater or lesser extent, targeted at the economically inactive who wish to work. The New Deals should be seen not purely as active labor market measures in the traditional sense, but as one of two key elements of the United Kingdom government's wider strategy of "welfare to work" (the other key element of this strategy being a fundamental review and reform of the United Kingdom's tax and benefit system).

Each of the different New Deal measures involves different approaches and design features and a range of incentives and support structures. Participation in the New Deal for Young People and the New Deal for Long-term Unemployed is mandatory (with benefit sanctions for non-participants) for those in the relevant age group meeting the eligibility criteria, whilst participation in the other New Deals remains voluntary. A common feature across all the New Deals, however, is the focus on activation through individualized advice and guidance, delivered by personal advisers who identify support measures (including training, where appropriate) for participants and who provide support and assistance in job search.

All of the New Deals are explicitly seen by the government as employability measures which aim not only to affect short-term employment and unemployment rates, but also to increase the longer-term employability of the target client groups.

This section concentrates in particular on the New Deal for Young People which, as the largest and longest-standing of the New Deals, has to date been subject to more evaluation than the others (although we also draw on some evidence relating to the New Deal for Long-Term Unemployed).

The New Deal for Young People

The New Deal for Young People (NDYP) is the main plank in the United Kingdom's strategy for tackling youth unemployment and aims to offer employment or training, with support, to all unemployed young people before they flow into long-term unemployment. The objectives of the NDYP, as set out by the government,[1] were as follows:

- to place young unemployed people more rapidly into jobs;

- to reduce recruitment costs and employer prejudice;

- to improve work skills, experience, qualifications, motivation, self-esteem and job-search skills;

- to enable the individual to choose the most appropriate method of obtaining and keeping a job;

- to maintain and improve effective job search throughout the program.

When considering the role of the NDYP as an employability measure, however, it is important to stress that, despite its title, none of the elements of the NDYP are fundamentally new; rather, they are all variants of existing or previous measures implemented in the United Kingdom or elsewhere in recent decades. In particular, it incorporates elements of the supply-side approach to active labor market policy which became dominant in the mid-1980s/early-1990s (with an emphasis on training, job-search activity, etc.) alongside a return to more traditional demand-side active labor market measures (employer subsidies, non-market job-creation schemes, etc.). Partly because of this hybrid, composite nature, the program presents significant evaluation difficulties in disentangling the distinct impacts of its many elements.

Despite its origins in earlier approaches to active labor market policy, the NDYP is, however, innovative in the United Kingdom context for several reasons. In particular:

- *Size*: It is much larger in scale than previous in initiatives—the projected expenditure on the NDYP over 1997-2002 was planned by the government to be £3.16 billion. By January 2000, some 422,100 young people had started in the program and, as figure 5.1 below also shows, inflows into the program have stabilized at around 15,000-20,000 per month. The total number of participants in the program at any one time, having peaked in Summer 1999 at around 150,000 about a year after the national roll-out, is expected to fall to around 90,000.[2] The program is also comprehensive in the sense that all young people aged 18-24 who have been claiming Job-seekers' Allowance[3] for six months or more are covered by the program. In addition, a number of special groups (within this age range) are eligible for entry to the New Deal before six months of unemployment.[4]

- *Individualized support and guidance*: In common with the other New Deals, a key feature of the NDYP is that it embodies important elements of what the policy literature identifies as an individualized "pathway to integration." Thus, all participants enter an initial "Gateway" program, which lasts for up to four months (during which they continue to receive JSA) and which consists of intensive counseling, advice, guidance and training, focused on job search, basic skills (literacy and numeracy) and personal problems which impact on the participant's employability. This support is delivered by New Deal Personal Advisers (NDPAs) from the public employment service. The Gateway aims to support as many as possible of the participants directly into unsubsidized jobs on the regular labor market and to prepare the remainder for the various options on the main phase of the New Deal itself.

- *Package of options*: Unlike the previous "one size fits all" approach of active labor market measures in the United Kingdom, the New Deal offers those young people without an unsubsidized job a choice amongst four options,[5] the choice depending on an assessment of their skills and needs:

  1. a subsidized job with an employer in the regular labor market (for six months); this option also includes, since July 1998, a variant under which the participant can opt for self-employment with financial support;

  2. six months' work as part of the Environment Task Force (essentially this is a job-creation program in environmental work);

  3. six months' work with an employer in the voluntary (charitable) sector;

  4. (for those without qualifications at NVQ level 2), full-time education and training for up to 12 months without loss of benefit.

- *A strong element of "activation"*: Those who refuse to participate in any of the above options following the Gateway period may have benefit sanctions applied to them. Participants at all stages of the program are expected, throughout, to be engaged in active job search; equally, it is the intention that the employment service and other agencies should be providing advice, guidance and job-search support to program participants throughout their period of participation.

Figure 5.1
New Deal for Young People—Entrants, Participants, and Leavers (monthly)

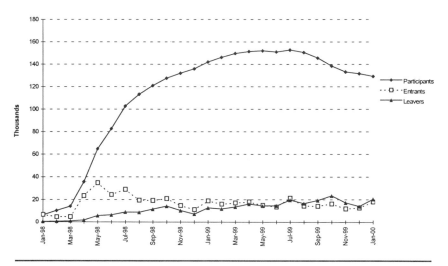

Source: DfEE, "New Deal for Young People and Long-Term Unemployed People aged 25+," Statistics, *DfEE Statistical First Release, SFR 10/2000*, 30 March 2000, London, Department for Education and Employment, 2000 (own calculations).

Finally, it should be noted that if a young person completes or leaves an option but has still not obtained employment, he/she can enter a further period of support, known as the "follow-through" period, during which he/she receives further intensive job-search support and may be redirected towards one of the four main New Deal options or, in a minority of cases, he/she may return to the Gateway period.

The New Deal for Long-term Unemployed Adults (25+)

The New Deal for Long-term Unemployed (NDLTU) aged 25 and over is a smaller, less complex program than the NDYP, although the two programs share several key features. It is smaller, because the client group (persons aged 25 and over, who have been unemployed and in receipt of JSA for two or more years)[6] is smaller than that for the NDYP. Broadly speaking, the program consists of three main elements:

- a series of regular advisory interviews with New Deal Personal Advisers, which may last for up to six months;

- access to a subsidized job option with an employer;

- access to a college-based education and training option for up to 12 months;

- participants may enter options 2 and 3 at any stage after six weeks of participation.

In addition, clients have access to the full range of existing training and job-search support provision for the long-term unemployed (most of which can be accessed after six months' employment).

Like the NDYP, the NDLTU has a mandatory element, although in the national program introduced in June 1998 only the advisory interview stage is compulsory. By contrast, under the so-called November pilots (introduced in pilot areas in November 1998), all stages of the program are compulsory. The November pilots tested a variety of alternative options (including access to the program at 18 months of unemployment rather than two years and a more intensive and comprehensive support package, more similar in some respects to that provided under the NDYP). The government has recently announced (March 2000) that as from April 2001 some elements of the November pilots will be introduced on a national basis, notably the extension of compulsory participation, earlier entry to

Figure 5.2
New Deal for Long-Term Unemployed Adults (25+)—
Entrants, Participants, and Leavers (monthly)

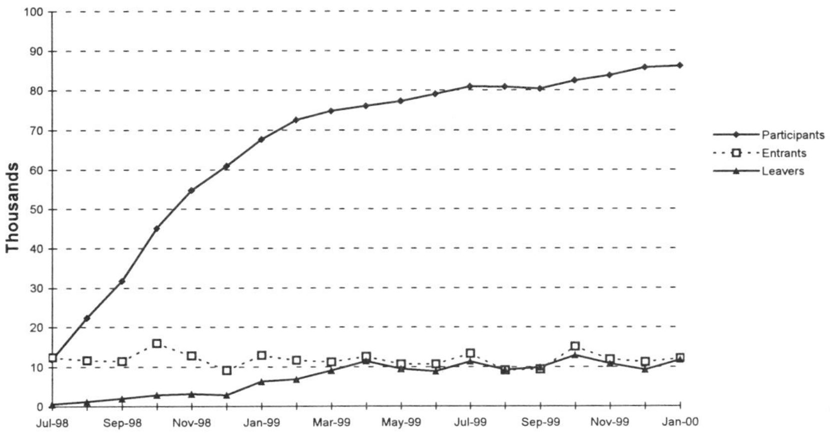

Source: DfEE, 2000 (own calculations).

the program (after 18 months' unemployment), and the inclusion of a structured Gateway stage, similar to that under the NDYP. This represents a major extension of the program, and it should be noted that this extension was introduced before the availability of in-depth evaluation evidence for the existing NDLTU and the November pilot variations became available.

Looking at the program to date, as figure 5.2 shows, by the end of January 2000 just over 250,000 long-term unemployed persons had started in the program, 140,700 of whom have left, and the program has settled down to a level of 80,000-90,000 participants at any one time.

Evaluation Findings to Date

The New Deals are also innovative in the United Kingdom context in that they have been subject to a more comprehensive and rigorous process of monitoring and evaluation than has been the case with any previous labor market programs. Of particular note is the fact that the evaluation strategy is taking place at a number of levels. Thus, in the case of the NDYP, the most extensively evaluated of the various New Deals, research is under way in examining the effect of the program on the employment/unemployment of the individual in the target groups, the effects on employers, the aggregate impact on unemployment, the net effects on the public exchequer, as well as broader macroeconomic and social impacts. The evaluation evidence emerging in the first 18 months of the program has been usefully summarized in a recent review conducted on behalf of the employment service,[7] and this review and other evaluation studies are drawn on in this article.

The New Deal for Young People

Even in the case of the NDYP, however, given the relative newness of the program (implemented nationally in April 1998), the monitoring and evaluation findings available to date tend to concentrate on processes and on short-term outcomes from the program. Evidence on longer-term impacts, essential for assessing the effectiveness of the program as an employability measure, will not emerge for several years. Inevitably, therefore, one's judgment on the program as an employability measure must be provisional, although there is an attempt, where possible, to draw attention to indicators of employability emerging from the evidence so far available.

Quality of support provided. As noted above, one of the key distinguishing features of the NDYP has been the intensive, customized, one-to-one support which is provided to all participants, especially during the Gateway stage, by a system of NDPAs. Early studies of the Gateway process at the pilot stage of the program suggested that the system of personal advisers was working well and that the client group had a positive attitude to this aspect of the program, but concern was also raised that the quality of this support might deteriorate as the number of New Deal participants expand to its maximum level.[8] More recent evaluation evidence has reinforced this concern, and the question clearly arises as to whether, despite the large resources available for the program, an employability program such as this one, which is dependent on high- quality intensive individual support, can effectively be delivered on a mass, nationwide scale. As Hasluck (2000) notes,

> The evaluation evidence points to the absolutely pivotal role of the NDPA in the process. The continuity and the form of support offered by NDPAs distinguishes the NDYP from what went before it. The relationship between client and the NDPA is crucial in determining the way in which the NDYP process develops for the young person. As the program has expanded in numbers, the pressure on NDPA caseloads has increased. One consequence of this appears to be that NDPA support falls off markedly during the options period and is very patch during follow-through.[9]

It is also worth noting that Walsh et al., 1999 found that a key reason for the relative failure to achieve placements into unsubsidized rather than subsidized jobs (see following) was a mismatch between participants' perceptions of their own "job-readiness" and those of employers, and the authors noted a common failure of NDPAs to confront these differences of perception and to ensure appropriate matches between employer expectations and client characteristics. It is clear that this issue is crucial in ensuring high levels of employer participation in the program.

Entry to employment. At the outset of the New Deal, the government's planning assumption (see House of Commons, 1998) was that around 40 percent of Gateway participants would directly enter an unsubsidized job on leaving the Gateway, rather than one of the subsidized New Deal options. As Figure 5.3 below shows, however, the planning assumption has not been fully met in practice; indeed, the share of Gateway leavers entering unsubsidized employment has tended to fall over time, as the program has expanded to its maximum size, and it is currently running at only 20-25 percent.

Also of concern is the fact that the proportion leaving the Gateway for the (subsidized) employment option has also tended to fall over time, so that by January 2000 only 3 percent of Gateway leavers were entering this option. This is of concern because, of all the options, those on the employment option are most likely to enter unsubsidized employment on leaving an option.[10] It is not yet clear from the evaluation data how far this reflects a "selection effect" (i.e., those on the employment option are likely to be the more "employable" or "job-ready" participants and more likely to be preferred by employers) with a significant "deadweight" element and how far it is an impact of the scheme (i.e., the employment option has a greater impact on subsequent employability than the other options). It is likely, however, that both effects are relevant.[11]

Additionally, however, it seems that the employment option may be more effective in leading to subsequent unsubsidized employment than the other options offered. This is consistent with the exist-

Figure 5.3
New Deal for Young People: Leavers from the Gateway
Stage by Immediate Destination

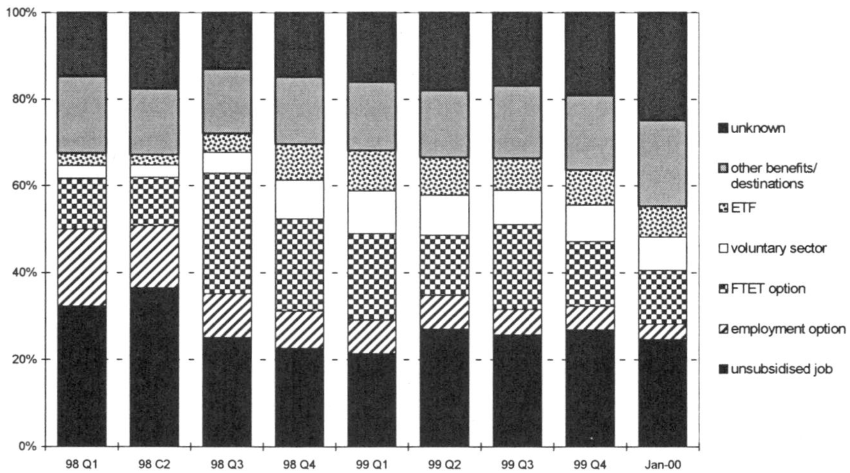

Source: DfEE, 2000 (own calculations).

ing national and international evidence on active labor market policies, which suggests that "market-oriented" measures which offer interventions as close as possible to "real world" experience coupled with occupationally relevant training have larger employability impacts than do measures based predominantly on classroom training and/or "make work" job creation schemes (as in the FTET and environmental task force options of the New Deal).[12]

As Hasluck, 2000 notes,

Elements of the NDYP, namely the subsidized employment option, embody an approach to labour market intervention sometimes referred to as "jobs first," while other elements are more conventional in that they seek to address perceived barriers to employment by providing training to overcome the barriers (lack of basic skills, ineffective job search, lack of qualifications) before securing a job. It is still too early to establish the long-term outcomes of the program. However, outcomes from the employment option appear to lend weight to the "jobs first" approach. Of those who enter a subsidized job placement, a very high proportion subsequently remained in employment at the end of the option or enter a job from follow-through fairly quickly thereafter. NDYP clients on FTET and, especially, those working in the voluntary sector or ETF tended to remain on the NDYP after options and leave follow-t' .ough at a relatively slow rate. While this difference could result from a selection of the most employable for subsidized employment (self-selection or selection by NDPAs), the early results of the evaluation provide *prima facie* evidence of the relative effectiveness of the subsidized job route to enhanced employability and an exit from the NDYP.

The declining shares of those leaving the Gateway directly for unsubsidized employment and those leaving for the subsidized employment option mean that taking all leavers from the program to-

Figure 5.4
Immediate Destinations on Leaving the New Deal for Young People

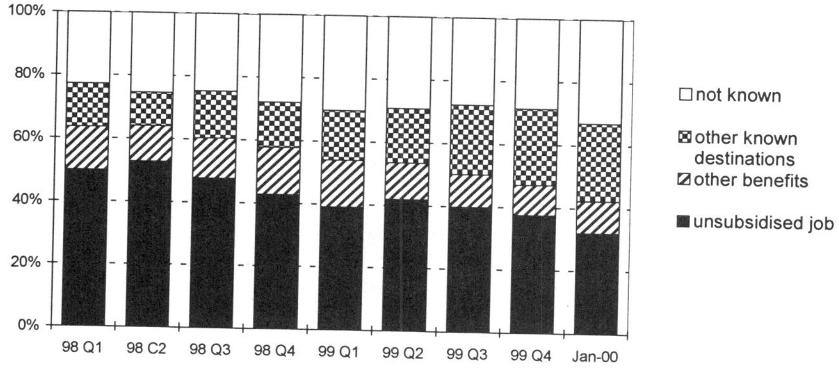

Source: DfEE, 2000 (own calculations).

gether (irrespective of whether they left from the Gateway stage or from the options stage or later) the share entering unsubsidized employment has tended to fall. See Figure 5.4.

It is also worth noting that the declining performance of the program (in terms of the proportion of leavers entering unsubsidized employment) has occurred in parallel with, and despite, an overall improvement in labor market prospects in the United Kingdom.

Also clear from Figures 5.3 and 5.4 is the fact that, whether one looks simply at leavers from the Gateway or leavers from the program as a whole, the proportion leaving for "unknown" destinations is significant and growing. Thus, over a quarter of leavers from the Gateway have unknown destinations, and this has increased over time. It remains unclear how many of these people have found jobs or who are "dropping out" for other reasons at the stage where they move from the Gateway to one of the mandatory full-time options of the scheme, under the threat of benefit sanctions for non-participation.[13] Research is under way to identify the destinations of this group, but it is clearly crucial in assessing the longer-term impact of this part of the United Kingdom's "welfare to work" strategy, to establish whether those leaving "welfare" as a result of the program

Figure 5.5
18-24 Year Olds Entering Employment from the New Deal (cumulative)

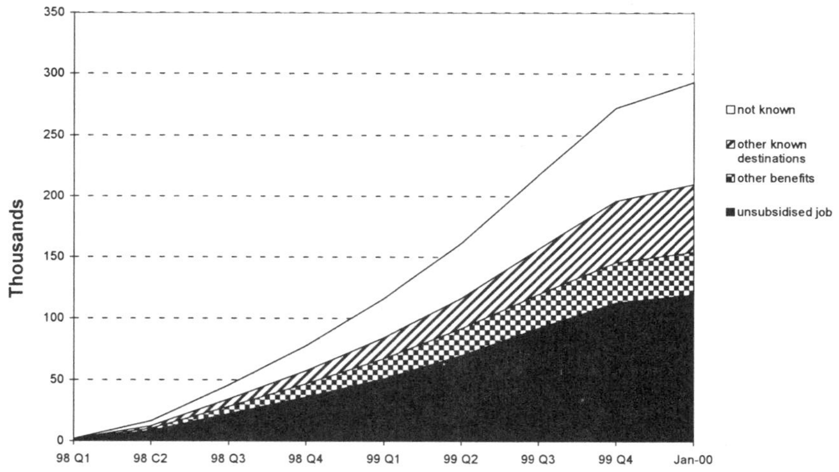

Source: DfEE, 2000 (own calculations).

are indeed entering "work," or whether some of them (faced with possible loss of benefit) are simply dropping out of the system into poverty, crime or the black economy.

At the outset of the program, the government stated an overall objective that the scheme would lead to some 250,000 young people entering employment during the government's first term. As can be seen from Figure 5.5, the program seems to be on course to meet this objective in a global sense, as over 190,000 participants from the program had obtained jobs by the end of January 2000.

Some caveats need to be put forward, however:

- First, in attributing job entry to program participation, one needs to take account of deadweight and possible displacement effects. No robust estimates of these are currently available, although a short-term macroeconomic simulation of the impact of the program on the stock of unemployment has been undertaken.[14] This showed that during the first year of the program deadweight was approximately 50 percent, i.e., that approximately 50 percent of those leaving unemployment via the NDYP would have done so in the absence of the program and that there was little evidence of any significant impact on other groups through substitution or displacement effects. If it can be sustained over time, this represents a relatively good performance, compared with previous active labor market measures in the United Kingdom, particularly given that the program was introduced at a time of a relatively tight labor market and falling unemployment, when deadweight might be expected to be relatively high. It should, of course, be noted that the impact of the program on unemployment is not the same as its impact on employment (typically it will be greater, as a proportion of those leaving the program go to non-employment destinations, such as economic inactivity, education or training). It is likely, therefore, that the impact of the program on employment (net of deadweight) is less than its impact on unemployment. Anderton et al. suggest that approximately two-thirds of those leaving unemployment as a result of the program (i.e., those who would not have left unemployment without the program) go into jobs.

- A key factor in assessing the impact of the NDYP clearly relates to the sustainability of the jobs entered by those leaving the scheme. The official data make a distinction between "sustained" jobs entered by scheme participants, on the one hand, and "short-term" jobs, on the other hand. Sustained jobs are defined as jobs lasting more than 13 weeks (i.e., in cases where the individual does not return to claim JSA or to transfer to another option under the program within 13 weeks. By any standard, 13 weeks can be seen as a very conservative definition of a sustained job. National data from the Labour Force Survey show that, with some cyclical fluctuation, the proportion of people in employment who stay in their jobs for less than three months is only around 4-6 percent. The fact that, as Figure 5.5 shows, some 27 percent of those entering employment from the NDYP end up keeping their jobs for less than three months suggests that, even allowing for higher-than-average job turnover rates among young people, the employment found by NDYP participation is disproportionately at the "unstable" end of the spectrum. It remains an open question at the present stage whether these high turnover jobs nevertheless generate enhanced employability for participants in the sense of providing an entry point to an improved career trajectory for these young people.

Figure 5.5 shows further that a proportion of those counted as having found "sustained" employment are in subsidized employment. On the assumption that Anderton et al.'s finding of 50 percent deadweight applies equally to the different categories of employment (detailed evidence to the contrary is not available), then looking only at "sustained" and unsubsidized jobs it can be seen that these account for 119,800 of the 191,600 young people who have entered jobs through the NDYP, and if half of these are deadweight it can be concluded that 59,900 (or 31 percent of the total) have entered sustained, unsubsidized jobs, but would not have done so in the absence of the program. Whilst not a negligible total, this figure suggests the need for caution in drawing strong conclusions about the positive employability impacts of the program, on the basis of the short-term evidence currently available, and points strongly to the need to await the results of the longitudinal tracking studies of NDYP participants which are currently under way.

The New Deal for the Long-Term Unemployed (25+)

To date, evaluation evidence from the NDLTU is even more limited than that available for the NDYP, and most of the existing evidence on the national program and the November pilots is qualitative in nature[15] and does not permit in any representative sense robust assessments of even the short-term impact of the program.

Comparing the initial monitoring data from the NDLTU with those available for the NDYP, however, it can be seen from Figure 5.6 that a slightly smaller proportion of NDLTU participants enter unsubsidized employment following the initial interview stage of the program than is the case for the NDYP, although unlike the latter the proportion has not been falling over time, and in recent months the proportion entering unsubsidized jobs is rather similar. Given the less intensive nature of the support offered under the NDLTU (although the intensity is to increase under the recent reform of the program) and the more disadvantaged nature of the client group, this performance is, on the face of it, encouraging (although at the time of writing there is no evidence as to the extent of deadweight in the NDLTU). The other notable feature is the smaller proportion of those who leave the initial stage for "unknown" destinations, compared with the NDYP, reflecting perhaps the fact that after the initial interview stage subsequent options under the NDLTU have not been mandatory, and the benefit sanctions incorporated in the NDYP have not been applied (although again, compulsion is to be extended under the recently announced revisions to the program, and it will be interesting to see whether this leads to an increase in the rate of "disappearance" of participants).

Figure 5.6
The New Deal for Long-Term Unemployed: Leavers from Advisory Interview Stage by Immediate Destination

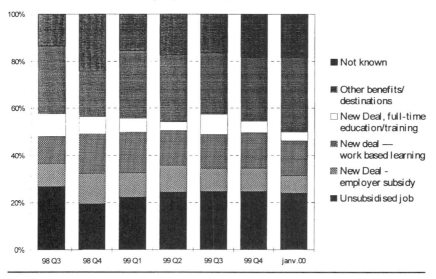

Source: DfEE, 2000 (own calculations).

Finally, Figure 5.7 shows that by the end of January 2000, 35,950 people had entered employment from the NDLTU, of which 84 percent are "sustained" jobs and 64 percent are unsubsidized, sustained jobs. The comparable figures for the NDYP are 73 percent and 62.5 percent, which again, given the more disadvantaged nature of the client group, suggests a relatively strong performance of the NDLTU, although in the absence of estimates of deadweight, etc. a full comparison between the two programs cannot be made. However, this also needs to be offset against the much smaller proportion of entrants to the scheme who had entered employment of any type (around 15 percent of NDLTU participants by the end of January 2000, compared with around 45 percent of NDYP participants, but again strict comparisons are not possible, given that the NDLTU is a more recent scheme, and the proportion is likely to rise over time—the authors were unable from the published monitoring data to make comparisons of similar entry cohorts from the two schemes).

Figure 5.7
25+ Year Olds Entering Employment from the New Deal for
Long-Term Unemployed (cumulative)

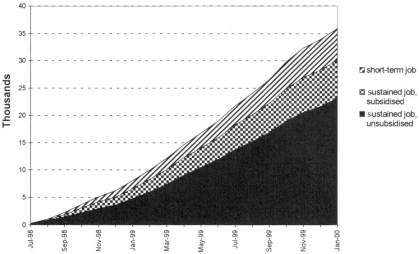

Source: DfEE, 2000 (own calculations).

Conclusions

It is clear that the various New Deals represent a major shift in active labor market policy in the United Kingdom in terms of the increased scale of intervention; the much greater degree of individualized support provided; and the wide menu of options offered, incorporating both supply—and demand-side measures.

As this discussion of the emerging evidence on the New Deals for Young People and for the Long-Term Unemployed has shown, however, it is too early to draw conclusions about whether these programs represent effective long-term measures for enhancing employability. Whilst there are encouraging signs in terms of the numbers of young people entering employment, relatively low deadweight (compared with previous measures), and positive qualitative evidence regarding the quality of the interventions provided, some major concerns remain. These relate, in particular, to:

- levels of "drop-out" to unknown destinations—there is a clear need for a better understanding of which participants "disappear" from the program and what happens to them;

- the sustainability of the employment entered by program participants and whether the short-term jobs obtained by many participants will effectively enhance longer-term employability;

- whether the high quality of individualized support offered by the New Deals can be maintained as the programs are expanded;

- whether the initially positive impacts of the program can be maintained in less favorable overall labor market conditions; and

- whether employer participation in the programs can be maintained and extended.

Flexcurity in the Netherlands

Wim Zwinkels and Marjolein Peters

Flexibility and Employability

Flexibility and employability are two factors that played an important role in the discussion on the future of the Dutch labor market. The concepts of flexibility and employability were both put on the Dutch political agenda by employers: flexibility in the 1980s, employability in the 1990s. They were each seen as critical factors for the adaptability and hence competitiveness of firms. Trade unions were suspicious at first, but gradually came to recognize the advantages of flexibility (reconciliation of work and personal life) and employability (training as reinforcement of the labor market position) for workers. The Dutch government supported the two notions, although it left much to the social partners when it came to putting them into practice.

Some definitions. Flexibility has an internal and an external dimension. Within both dimensions, a distinction can be made between a numerical and a functional form. The following figure provides an overview of these dimensions and forms.

Employability is the most universally employable term found in the labor market dictionary. Factually, the term's definition customarily implies that employees are more employable if and when they are able and inclined to work at various intra- and extra-organizational locations. Increasingly, human resource management (HRM) symbolizes competency management. The interrelation between the internal and external labor market is of great significance in this respect. As for the external labor market, selection is based on such

Figure 5.8
Dimensions and Forms of Flexible Utilization of
Work and Variable Remuneration

External numerical	**External functional**
• Fixed-term contracts	• Detachment
• Temporary work	• Free-lance work
• Labour pools	• Home work
• Stand-by staff	• Subcontracting
• Internal detachment	
Internal numerical	**Internal functional**
• Working overtime	• Incidental change of duties
• Flexible rosters	• Task enlargement
• Part-time work	• Task enrichment
• Shift work	• Transfers
• Variable work hours	• Function rotation

Source: Delsen and Visser, 1999.[16]

Figure 5.9
Employability Layers

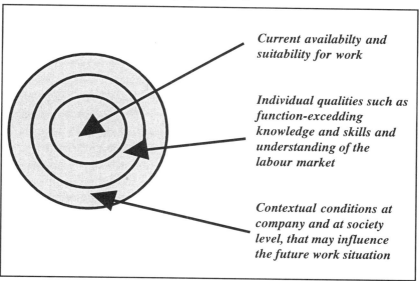

*Current availabilty and
suitability for work*

*Individual qualities such as
function-excedding
knowledge and skills and
understanding of the
labour market*

*Contextual conditions at
company and at society
level, that may influence
the future work situation*

Source: Based on Thijssen (2000).[17]

constant competencies as capacities and personality characteristics, while experimenting with such modifiable competencies as know-how and behavioral attitudes marks selection for the internal labor market. Flexible attitudes, self-autonomy, learning capacity and personal entrepreneurship constitute major ingredients as regards successful careers.

Employability is nowadays seen as comprising both the individual and contextual factors that influence the future labor market position on a certain labor market (see Figure 5.9).

Historical context. The definitions of the two concepts have changed considerably through time. Thijssen[18] distinguishes three phases in the historical development of the flexible deployment of workers: flexibility of society, flexibility of organization and flexibility of workers. The three final decennia of the previous century are characterized by these three forms successively.

If there was such a notion as employability in the 1970s, it was applied to people outside the labor market. The government helped the weaker groups to enter the labor market. Having a job generally meant having lifelong employment.

During the 1980s, companies strove to increase their flexibility. Within their companies, they attempted to introduce flexible working time and flexible working hours, as well as an easier transfer of employees from one function to another. Employability predominantly meant training of the company's core workers. At the same time, external flexibilization was sought in flexible work contracts and the hiring of knowledge on an ad-hoc basis.

Both the government and its social partners stimulated and facilitated external (numeric) flexibility in the 1990s. Employers looked for external and gradually also internal mobility of staff. Promotion and career within one company on the basis of seniority were no longer self-evident. In the 1990s, the notion of employability became a concept relating to the individual: a labor market tool for people who find themselves in a society that stresses individual responsibility and offers progressively less protection.

The ever-tightening labor market in the Netherlands has contributed greatly to a change in the attitude of the social partners towards employability. Employers have now become anxious to keep their personnel and therefore prefer to give them training in such a way that it will bind them to their company. As a result, they have become more reserved towards employability. Trade unions in turn have now embraced the notion of employability, because they recognize the opportunities it offers to workers.

The following section examines the situation with regard to flex work in the Netherlands. The next two sections describe the Flexcurity Act and the first effects it has had on temporary workers, employers and temporary work agencies. In the final section, the thesis that employability is gradually superseding that of flexibility is put forward.

Flex Work in the Netherlands

Roughly 10 percent of Dutch employees had a flex job as their main job in 1998. More than one-third of them were temporary workers. These flex workers comprise stand-in staff, zero-hours staff and staff with similar contracts, stand-by staff, workers contracted through temporary employment agencies and employees holding fixed-term contracts.

Roughly 11 percent of the jobs in the Netherlands in 1999 were flex jobs.[19] In Figure 5.10, employees holding temporary contracts who foresee that they will receive a permanent contract are counted as those with "permanent jobs."

Figure 5.10
Flexible Workers in the Netherlands

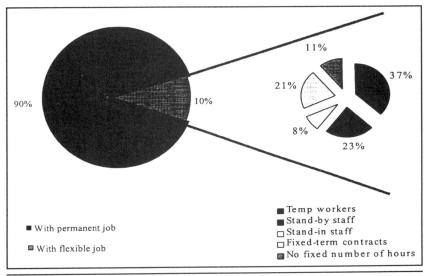

Source: CBS Statistics Netherlands, *Enquête Beroepsbevolking* (Labour Force Survey).
Note: This labor force survey includes only people working 12 hours per week or more.
In case a person holds more than one job, the job with the most hours is included.

Development of flex work. Over the past decades, labor flexibilization increased steadily. In 1992, 7.6 percent of the employees were flex workers. Their share had increased to more than 10 percent in 1998.

Preliminary CBS figures for 1999 and for the first quarter of 2000 show that the share of flex jobs is somewhat diminishing. In data from the Organization for Strategic Labour Market Research (OSA) coming from a panel survey, several indications can also be found that the number of flexible employment contracts is decreasing. Owing to the tight labor market situation, (potential) employees will be better equipped to realize their preferences. The findings of an ROA survey,[20] for instance, reveal that school-leavers are increasingly being offered either permanent jobs or the prospects thereof. Incidentally, even employers themselves seem to be more restrained as regards recruiting employees on a temporary-contract basis. Given the high mobility among this category, too high numbers of flexible employees might be disadvantageous as regards continuity of business management and intra-organizational knowledge transfer. Fur-

Table 5.1
Flex Work in the Netherlands, 1992-99

	1992	1993	1994	1995	1996	1997	1998	1999
Total number of employees (x 1,000)*	5258	5261	5222	5357	5459	5644	5874	6072
Share of flexible workers (%), of which	7.6	7.5	8.1	8.9	9.9	10	10.3	9.4
Temporary workers	1.9	1.9	2.2	2.8	3.4	3.7	3.8	3.5
Stand-by staff	1.5	1.5	1.7	2	2.1	2.1	2.3	1.8
Fixed-term contracts	2.1	2.3	2.4	2.4	2.3	2.4	2.2	3.4 a)
No fixed number of hours	1.3	1.1	1.2	1.1	1.1	1.1	1.2	

Source: *Enquête Beroepsbevolking*, CBS-Statistics Netherlands (Labour Force Survey).
Note: The Dutch labour force survey includes only people working 12 hours per week or more. In case a person holds more than one job, the job with the most hours is included. All percentages: share of total number of employees.
a):   For 1999 only a combined figure is available for fixed-term contracts and workers with no fixed number of hours.

thermore, costs will be incurred in the event of continuous recruitment and training of temporary employees.

Internal and external flexibility. The figures quoted above refer to what is called external numerical flexibility. The OSA data also allow a comparison of various forms of labor flexibility. De Lange and Thunissen[21] observe from these data that some forms of internal numerical flexibility are increasing (e.g., overtime work), whereas others are somewhat decreasing (notably, irregular working hours and shift work). According to them, functional flexibility of workers is gradually increasing. In total, they conclude that a shift is taking place from external to internal flexibilization.

Between 1996 and 1998, rising numbers of employees deemed themselves flexible.[22] The share of employees who were often activated in another division or position rose from 14 percent to 17 percent between 1996-98. The highest degree of multi-utility materialized among employees aged between 25-50 years commanding medium educational backgrounds; yet over the past years, multi-utility rose most vigorously among older and highly trained employees. Besides this performance-related flexibility, changes in position and course enrolment were rising also.

Reasons for the high share of flex workers. From the enterprises' view, owing to several trends, there was an increasing demand for flexible labor, viz.:

- ever-increasing competition: focusing on price and quality (due to globalization and liberalization of goods and services markets), competition increasingly transpired in the international arena;

- continuous changes as regards customers' needs in respect of type and characteristics of products and services;

- continuous changes in technology domains that spurred modified production processes, as well as changes in the composition of product ranges and service packages.

The flex labor volume was also affected by such supply-side factors as individualization, flexibility, combination of work with family-care tasks and increased female labor participation. Also restrictions to study funding had a positive impact on the supply of labor.

The Dutch flexible labor market is huge. Compared to overall employment figures, the Netherlands is second to none as regards accommodating the highest numbers of temporary employees. Besides the aforementioned general reasons, there are characteristic factors affecting the Netherlands in this respect; two of the major factors are elaborated hereinafter.

Firstly, the Dutch labor market is marked by high statutory protection against unemployment. Owing to this, employers face difficulties to shed surplus staff. If the expected working period is brief, wage costs of flexible labor are lower than those of permanent labor. Secondly, already from the early 1960s onward, temporary employment agencies in the Netherlands were granted operating licences. In other European countries, the institutional emergence of temporary employment agencies materialized at a later stage.

The Flexcurity Act

The importance of flex work, both as a source of employment and for the competitiveness of companies, prompted a change in

Dutch labor legislation. The Flexcurity Act, effective 1 January 1999, aims to balance two different interests. On the one hand, the Act establishes more job and social protection for flex workers. On the other hand, it gives employers more possibilities for a flexible deployment of workers.

Already prior to the Flexcurity Act adoption, commotion arose. In public opinion, the Act tended to be associated with protection of flex workers and, hence, a deterrent to the use of flex work by companies. Flex workers had, for instance, allegedly been made redundant in anticipation of the Act, and changes in employment contracts had been effected. Moreover, schools allegedly had to send entire classes home in the event of teacher absenteeism, since they would not dare to call up substitute lecturers fearing they would have to be offered permanent employment contracts. On the other hand, very expensive soccer stars were allegedly permitted to terminate contracts while observing a one-month notice term and were free to move on to other (foreign) clubs without any transfer fees involved. Extensive evaluation of the Act was foreseen in order to monitor such effects, amongst others.

Better Protection

- *The existence of an employment agreement*

The Flexcurity Act clarifies whether an employment agreement exists in the case of flexible labor. According to the Act, an employment contract materializes if and when an employee assumes paid labor every week or minimally 20 hours a month for a period of three months, while the employer must now produce evidence that the employment relation does not qualify for the conditions to grant an employment contract.

- *Contract extension*

Prior to the Act's adoption, if a temporary employment contract was extended within 31 days maximum, this new employment contract did not terminate automatically. A permanent employment contract automatically existed once a second employment contract was signed. Employers could only terminate the contract by applying for a dismissal permit granted by the public employment service and by observing a term of notice.

The modified legislation stipulates that an employer may offer several subsequent temporary employment contracts to an employee. Temporary employment contracts will automatically be converted into permanent contracts, and employees will be entitled to dismissal protection only once the cases stated hereinafter occur:

- If three subsequent temporary employment contracts have been entered successively or within a three-month span, the fourth contract will thus automatically entail a permanent employment contract.

- If the duration of subsequent temporary employment contracts is longer than 36 months on aggregate, i.e., including any intervals of a maximum of three months, as soon as the entire working relation consumes 36 months on aggregate the temporary employment contract will be converted into a permanent one. This may coincide with the start of a new contract if all previous contracts totalled 36 months on aggregate. If the 36-month span is exceeded during an employment contract term, then that contract will be converted instantaneously into a permanent employment contract.

The rule also applies to temporary employment contracts offered by employers who act as respective successors as regards an employee's tasks. For example, this may pertain to cases where a worker contracted by a temporary employment agency initially works for an employer via that agency and is subsequently recruited directly by that employer.

The Act stipulates a transitory measure; viz. temporary employment contracts entered before 1 January 1999 that had not terminated by that date and met the qualifying conditions will not be converted into a permanent employment contract.

Increasing Flexibility

On the other hand, the Flexcurity Act contains a number of provisions that allow employers a greater flexibility in the utilization of labor.

- *Trial period*

The trial period in employment contracts used to be two months, regardless of the type of contract. The Act stipulates that in the case of temporary contracts this period will be limited to one month for contracts with a duration of less than two years.

- *Contract extension*

The protection against dismissal in the case of extension of a temporary contract has been lifted.

- *Term of notice*

Previously, the term of notice depended on various factors: period of wage payment, duration of employment and age. Currently, only the employment duration determines the term of notice for the employer. In the case of an employment contract (relation) of less than five years, the term of notice is one month. This period goes up to four months in case an employee has been employed for 15 years or longer. For employees, the term of notice is always one month. Trial periods can be extended in writing. Shortening can only be agreed in collective agreements.

- *Dismissal*

If an employer wants to dismiss an employee, he or she needs to ask the public employment service for permission. The Flexcurity Act makes the route through the employment service more attractive for employers, because:

- this procedure is shortened;

- completion of this procedure gives the employer the right to decrease the term of notice period by one month (as long as one month always remains);

- the employer may terminate the contract in case of illness of the employee, provided his or her illness started after the employment service received the request for dissolution of the contract.

The Situation of Temporary Workers

A temporary work agreement between a temporary worker and a temporary work agency is now considered an employment agreement. After six months, all regulations regarding an employment agreement fully apply. During the first six months, however, some specific rules exist:

- contrary to other fixed-term contracts, more than three temporary work agreements can be concluded without this automatically leading to conversion into a fixed-term contract;

- the temporary agency and the temporary worker can agree in writing that the temporary work agreement is dissolved in case the hiring company sends back the worker. On the other hand, temporary workers can quit their job at any time.

The Act allows employers and employees to diverge from the maximum terms mentioned in the Act. This possibility has already been used by workers and employers in the temporary work industry. The new collective agreement agreed upon by employers and employees, covering the 1999-2002 span and governing workers contracted by temporary employment agencies, comprises a phasing system stipulating that an increasing duration of a worker being contracted to work via a temporary employment agency entitles that worker to increasing privileges, which will eventually result in a permanent employment contract granted by the temporary employment agency. This phasing systems amongst others implies that:

- After six months. a temporary worker has the right to a training-needs interview and inclusion in a pension scheme. A percentage of the temporary fee is reserved for training of temporary workers by the temporary agencies.

- After one year, temporary workers will receive only contracts of at least three months. In addition, they will continue to be paid if no work is available during that period.

- After one and a half years and having worked with the same client of the temporary agency, the temporary worker is entitled to an open-ended contract with the temporary agency.

- Temporary workers who worked for the same agency but for different clients have the same right after three years.

Instead of the phase system, temporary agencies can also conclude a so-called chain contract with their workers. In that case, in principle no more than three fixed-term agreements can be concluded within a maximum period of three years. After that, an employment agreement will in principle enter into force assumed with the next agreement.

It should be noted that the above constitutes a global summary of the collective agreement. Many detailed provisions exist with regard to the calculation of working and non-working periods, for example.

Initial Effects of the Flexcurity Act

In its entirety, the Flexcurity Act has turned out to be very complicated. Not much is known as yet about the effects. The Ministry of Social Affairs and Employment commissioned a study into initial experience gained with the Act. The study comprised polls among relevant employees (i.e., flex workers), employers in general and temporary employment agencies. The polls were conducted two months after adoption of the Act. Since, at that stage, many cases qualified for the transitory measure stipulated and because no or hardly any concrete experience had been gained in respect of several elements of the Act, no conclusion may be drawn as regards the ultimate structural effects of the Flexcurity Act.

The impact on flex workers. Compared to the number of flex workers in the Netherlands, the number who actually encountered the impact of the Flexcurity Act was comparatively small, i.e., 45,000 employees approximately. Primarily, these entail stand-in staff who had not been called up, stand-in staff who had been referred to temporary employment agencies, temporary contract holders who had not been issued new contracts, temporary workers whose employment contracts had been terminated temporarily or who had been referred to temporary employment agencies, and workers contracted by temporary employment agencies with whom relations had been terminated. The major reason underpinning these disadvantageous effects entails that employers either did not want or were not in the position to offer permanent employment contracts.

Also, the number of flex workers encountering the Flexcurity Act in a positive way was small. Approximately 35,000 stand-in staff had been offered permanent employment contracts. The number of temporary employees who had been offered permanent employment contracts is estimated at 12,500.

The long-term effects depend on collective bargaining, avoidance behavior by employers (new constructions, adaptation of HRM policy) and labor market trends. Regarding the latter, the tight labor market limited the number of flex workers, since employers were more inclined to bind staff by means of permanent contracts.

Totalling 31 percent, demand for training among workers contracted by temporary employment agencies was low. In the first two months, 13 percent of the workers had had a training-demand interview. More than half of the temporary employment agencies introduced a retirement scheme. Those who had introduced a retirement scheme stated that, on average, the scheme covered one-third of the workers contracted. This applies to a greater extent to large rather than small enterprises.

The impact on employers. Employers primarily complained about compliance costs and discontinuity of the labor organization process. The direct effects of having to offer permanent employment contracts to those employees to whom they were not inclined to do so seem small, partly because they had already anticipated this situation. Remarkably, employers were not explicitly positive as regards changes in dismissal procedures and opportunities to offer more subsequent temporary employment contracts to the same employee.

However, there are also positive signals, in that one-fourth of the employers had adopted positive attitudes by then. They acknowledged the transparency of the Act and considered that they would handle staff more conscientiously.

The impact on temporary employment agencies. Most temporary employment agencies, too, initially rated the Flexcurity Act as negative, probably because in the recent past they did not have to observe any maximum temporary labor term in view of a policy marked by tolerance. Besides, occasionally, constructions had been employed so as to avoid maximum terms. Workers contracted by temporary employment agencies, for instance, had been offered interim temporary contracts by the contractor (client) and had subsequently been contracted anew on a temporary employment basis. The maximum temporary employment term had thus not been an insurmountable obstacle as such.

Presently, temporary employment agencies face the new rules governing training and retirement schemes. Various issues such as working-life antecedents have to be recorded.

In view of the tight labor market, temporary employment agencies probably would also have unfolded activities to bind staff to an increasing extent, even without adoption of the Flexcurity Act. As for the coming years, it will be even more difficult to recruit temporary workers. Besides, it is anticipated that the new rules will generate far-reaching changes in the areas of automation and administration, causing increased work-related pressure for organizations and, therefore, higher costs of temporary labor.

On the other hand, there are also temporary employment agencies that rated the Flexcurity Act as positive. Partly, this seems to be attributable to their view that the sector will now acquire a more positive image. Also the aspect of barring "con artists" is of significance.

Recently, temporary employment agencies have gained front-page publicity. According to them, many agencies have orders that are too irregular to offer permanent employment contracts if workers contracted by them have reached the phase-4 time span. Owing to this, according to a spokesperson of "collectively nervous agencies," flex workers are pooled en masse by temporary employment agencies. Flex workers are deliberately not being called up, since enterprises do not want to commit themselves. Therefore, this category of workers has to rely on unemployment benefits. Security has thus been altered to insecurity.

From Flexibility to Employability

As mentioned in the introduction to this section, flexibility and employability were both important points in the Dutch socioeconomic policies of the 1990s. The need for flexibility prompted the interest in employability, at first predominantly in terms of external flexibility and mobility. Flexibilization was the dictum in times of insecurity as regards economic progress, on the one hand, and an ample supply in the labor market, on the other. Presently, a shift seems to be materializing within the flexibilization arena, i.e., from external to internal flexibilization. The share of flex labor in total employment is stabilizing at a little more than 10 percent. Enterprises primarily attempt to enhance their flexibility by boosting the all-round utilization of permanent staff. The task of many mobility centres in organizations was enlarged to include the workers the organization wanted to keep within the company. It can be expected that in training the emphasis will become more on product/service and company related and that the acquisition of more general, transferable skills will not be encouraged.

The Flexcurity Act stimulates flexible labor by offering more possibilities for fixed-term contracts, additional room for temporary work and shortening the dismissal time. It may contribute to the employability of temporary workers, since these obtain a position similar to other workers after a certain time. The collective agreement of temporary workers provides for a training needs interview after six months already.

Flex labor has gained a major position in the Dutch labor market. However, the shortage of personnel draws employers' interest away from flexibility to employability. As a result, the effects of the Act may well be less positive than otherwise might have been the case. There is certainly no reason to assume that flex labor will pose a large-scale surrogate threat to regular labor.

As a final observation, it should be pointed out that the labor market situation—labor surpluses or shortages—may well turn out to be a far more dominant factor for the development of flexibility and employability in companies than the economic and social considerations usually brought forward.

Unemployment Traps in Belgium

Koen Van Den Heuvel

One of the main structural problems in the Belgian labor market is the low employment rate of relatively unskilled persons. In 1998, only 55 percent of the less-skilled persons between 25 and 59 years old (i.e., those who only finished lower secondary education) had a job, compared with 87 percent of the skilled workers. This low employment rate should be somewhat qualified, since "moonlighting" is not included in this estimate.

The existence of moonlighting and the low employment rate of the less skilled reflect the difficulties in creating and filling regular jobs in the less-skilled sector of the labor market. The problem of creating and filling the low-productivity jobs for the less skilled has proven very complex.

This section discusses in broad outline the problem of unemployment traps, which is only one facet—albeit very important—of the plight of the less skilled. After defining the unemployment trap as a phenomenon, certain types of unemployment traps and their causes will be highlighted. Then the Belgian situation will be described briefly, and some recent political initiatives designed to counteract these traps will be indicated.

Before considering the offer of less-skilled labor, one should first consider whether the demand for low-productivity jobs in the labor market is sufficient.

The Demand for Low-Productivity Jobs: The Productivity Trap

Creating low-productivity jobs in the normal circuit poses a problem for various reasons. Reference is regularly made to the labor costs problem or, in other words, to the risk of a productivity trap: in some cases, low-productivity jobs are not sufficiently productive to allow the employer to cover the labor costs. The relatively low productivity of these jobs is inferior to the labor costs, the level of which is determined by pressure from special taxes and minimum wages or by the lowest pay scales, imposed through collective bargaining, which are often substantially higher than the minimum wage.

There is also a clear risk that capital will be substituted for labor. If the costs of labor rise at a faster pace than the costs of capital, the company management will be inclined to look for cheaper production processes, leading to the replacement of the "labor" factor of production by capital (for example, robots replacing assembly-line workers).

In some cases, the demand for jobs disappears when labor costs exceed marginal productivity. This phenomenon occurs when the cost of certain services that are strongly labor-intensive proves higher than the value that the users attach to such services (for example, maintenance work and gardening). In this case, capital is not used to replace labor, but the services are no longer required. Another possible outcome would be the shifting of certain services to the informal sector. Without pressure from special taxes, these services become affordable for the consumer.

The Labor Supply for Low-Productivity Jobs: The Unemployment Trap

Definition of the Unemployment Trap. Reasons for participating in the labor market are very complex. In fact, the choice between taking a job and remaining out of work is determined by financial factors, but also by other qualitative factors such as a perception of activities within, but also outside, the workplace, career prospects, the family situation, etc. Nevertheless, the financial incentive has a strong influence, even if the degree of importance varies from case to case. Thus, a young worker would accept a relatively low beginning salary if the job offers possibilities of a raise.

All these factors also play a part in the decision of whether or not to accept a low-productivity job. It is precisely for such jobs that the choice between taking a job and remaining jobless is most difficult. Since low-productivity jobs are usually low-salary jobs, there is indeed a risk that the financial incentive for accepting these jobs will prove too weak. Besides, it is among the workers normally slated for such jobs that the risk of insufficient interest is the greatest.

For those in low-productivity jobs, the unemployment trap risk can arise for a variety of reasons (financial, lack of interest, etc.) and the incentive for the job-seekers to look for and accept a job or some training may be lacking. The person in question may feel trapped by his or her dependence on welfare allowances; yet his/her quality of life would perhaps not improve by accepting a job.

The Types of Unemployment Traps and Their Causes. The term "unemployment trap" covers a number of aspects that deserve an explanation. In general, a distinction is made between two forms of unemployment traps, i.e., the financial trap and the non-financial trap.

- *The financial unemployment trap*

A financial unemployment trap refers to a situation in which accepting a job does not improve the worker's purchasing power, or betters it only slightly. The income from welfare benefits is relatively high in comparison with the income expected from work; in other words, the difference between the net income expected from work and the so-called "reservation" wage, i.e., the minimum wage for which the worker would accept a job, in some cases is negative.

Apart from the salary, other elements influence the labor supply and also contribute to determining the reservation wage. The factors that limit the labor supply have the effect of raising the reservation wage. Thus, the worker's reservation wage increases when:

- the worker's replacement income grows;

- financial assistance increases (e.g., larger family allowances, additional subsidies for health care, complementary payments for seniority, income guarantee payments, etc.) or supplementary payments are granted;

- the worker has fairly easy access to income from moonlighting;

- the initial investment costs (e.g., clothing, car, child care) for the worker to be able to accept a job increase;

- the worker's career prospects are low and/or the job is temporary.

In addition to the loss of social benefits, the sudden loss of complementary financial payments when one takes on a job, as well as the presumably unlimited duration of unemployment allowances, can also play an important role in the appearance of an unemployment trap. The experience of employment services confirms that the initial investment costs should not be underestimated. For a person who is dependent on welfare payments, investing in a new bicycle or a new car or looking for possible child care when taking on a new job becomes a problem, especially if it is only for a temporary job.

Another cause of financial unemployment traps is to be found in the relatively low level of net income from work. It is not so much the gross wage that is at the core of the problem. The application of the minimum legal wage and the minima, based on collective sectoral labor agreements which are usually higher, guarantees a base salary for the low-productivity jobs. Higher gross wages increase the labor cost of these jobs, augmenting the risk of productivity traps and thereby hindering the creation of such jobs. With an identical gross salary, for the lowest salaries the net income from work can be made more attractive if the tax and special tax on workers were adjusted for these wage categories. At present, a strong marginal tax pressure is felt at the passage from joblessness to a work situation, given that persons dependent on welfare enjoy a special tax treatment, while persons with a low-salary job are subject to the normal tax and special tax system (e.g., the workers' contributions to social security).

- *The non-financial unemployment trap*

A low financial incentive is not the only element that can keep the job-seeker dependent on welfare. Non-financial reasons can also influence the unemployed worker not to accept a job in the regular circuit. Thus, a policy aimed at reducing the risk of unemployment traps should not be approached from a purely financial angle, but rather from a broader perspective.

A lack of interest in obtaining a job can be due to various causes. Practical experiences of the employment services when placing and accompanying the unemployed (particularly the long-term unemployed) reveal that many factors curb their interest in working.

A first factor of considerable importance relates to the social and professional aptitudes of the unemployed worker. Some of them fail to find a job because their training level is too low and/or because their qualifications no longer correspond to the market's requirements. In Belgium, more than 40 percent of the working population has a diploma no higher than the lower secondary education level. Inadequate schooling is an important factor in the risk of becoming long-term unemployed. The need to increase the training opportunities for job-seekers is thus once again confirmed. Education, and particularly technical and vocational secondary education, should also be given greater consideration. Anyone leaving school should have a minimum starting qualification (i.e., a minimum of knowledge and social skills), so as to increase his/her chances for success in the labor market.

On the other hand, over-qualification is also a problem for hiring: applicants with relatively high qualifications have an advantage over less-qualified persons at the hiring stage, even though the job on offer does not require such high qualifications. In other respects, some unemployed lack, or no longer have, the appropriate attitudes to perform adequately in a regular job on the labor market, or they have asocial tendencies (for example, a lack of self-discipline at work). Furthermore, long-term unemployment can trigger psychological and social adaptation processes that cause discouragement and diminish the active search for a job. Frustrations born of the desire to work and the impossibility of finding a job can bring about a defense reaction on the part of the unemployed worker, which translates into a loss of interest in paid work and less frequent applications for jobs. Generally, this absence of professional motivation goes along with an inadequate education and, in some families, the lack of interest is transmitted from generation to generation. To break this vicious circle is difficult and doubtless requires an intensive individual integration effort.

The family situation can also influence the availability of an unemployed worker. Some unemployed, especially women, are prisoners of unemployment or of a dependent situation regarding welfare payments, because these payments are indispensable to their families (e.g., single-parent families with children, ailing parents). Developing social infrastructure, in general, and child-care facilities, in particular, could increase significantly the availability of this group for work.

On the other hand, the quality of low-salary jobs plays a role in the decision of whether or not to accept a job. Some low-salary jobs can be difficult and have to be performed at irregular hours. A constantly greater flexibility is demanded of the worker who accepts an "atypical" job, forcing him/her to readjust the rhythm and organization of his/her life. In addition, many low-paying jobs are part time; thus, the financial incentive to leave a situation of dependence on welfare is minimal. Some unemployed are unwilling to reorganize their whole lives in order to take an atypical part-time job.

Too great a geographical distance between the demand and the supply of work also restricts the availability of certain unemployed workers. In Belgium, a good number of job-seekers display very little geographical mobility, which can be explained by cultural differences, the limited availability of public transport, and the high costs of moving.

Finally, there is also an "administrative" unemployment trap, linked to the fear of losing the security of welfare payments. The unemployed person prefers the relative security of welfare dependence to the uncertainty of a new job. This generally stems from apprehensions that the unemployed worker will not be able to perform the work correctly, will not be well treated by his/her employer, or will not be paid regularly. In case of dismissal after being hired, the unemployed worker fears the complicated administrative processes required in order to regain the entitlement to welfare payments. There is the additional risk that the new welfare allowance may be lower than the previous one. This "administrative" trap can result in a refusal to accept a job, in particular when a temporary and/or precarious job is being considered. This deterrent comes more openly into play in the case of less-qualified persons who lack administrative know-how.

From these elements, it is clear that a policy aimed at reducing the risk of unemployment traps cannot be limited to a purely financial approach. The growth of financial incentives is not sufficient, although it does constitute an essential condition to encourage a greater number of welfare beneficiaries to take steps to enter the labor market.

How to Measure the Risk of a Financial Unemployment Trap

Measuring the financial traps proves to be a very complex exercise. The method most often used is the technique of standard simulations. This consists in calculating for certain types of household the gaps between the gross and the net income, in case of work and in case of no work, so as to make abundantly clear the net benefit of work. In the problem of measuring the financial unemployment traps, determining the increase in revenues needed to generate a sufficient financial incentive is an extremely important factor. It is impossible to set an absolute threshold of income growth above which there would be no risk of a financial trap. In any case, the risk of a financial trap is subjective and has a dynamic of its own: for some, a 2 percent raise in revenue constitutes a financial trap, while others would accept a job in those same conditions. Thus, a young worker will easily accept a job which represents only a slight increase in revenue, if the job offers favorable prospects.

In a recent study by the Superior Council on Employment (Conseil supérieur de l'Emploi), based on data from the Social Policy Centre (Centre de Politique sociale), the floor value of minimum increase in revenue was fixed at 15 percent. From this study, it is obvious that, when shifting from a situation of long-term unemployment (more than one year) to a full-time job, the financial incentive is not adequate for a one-parent household or for a household with maximum welfare allowances. Single persons, cohabitants and households receiving a minimum welfare allowance derive a sufficient financial advantage thereby. When they accept a part-time job, however, nearly all the types of household register only a limited gain in revenue from it.

It is difficult to determine exactly how many unemployed would be found in each specific category. The Superior Council, based on its own forecasts, concluded that at the beginning of 1998 a financial unemployment trap was a risk for a maximum of 95,000 heads of household, out of 125,000 heads of household unemployed for one year (78 percent of the total) and out of 285,000 unemployed workers with over one year of benefits (33 percent), when offered a full-time job at approximately the minimum wage. At the beginning of 1998, some 285,000 unemployed on benefits would have found the financial incentive too small when passing from long-term unemployment to a part-time job.

Political Initiatives

In view of the problem's complexity, a multifaceted approach is indicated if one wishes to advance in eliminating the unemployment traps. Reducing the financial unemployment traps is not enough, although it is essential for encouraging the persons who depend on welfare to look for and accept a job. In addition, long-lasting changes are necessary in terms of training, social infrastructure and administrative regulations (which require changes in the behavior both of the employers and of the workers).

Lacking any form of net income increase, the motivation would be limited for most of the welfare beneficiaries. It is therefore of utmost importance to widen the gap between welfare income and income from work. One possible way to fulfil this objective would be to lower the unemployment benefits. However, this is not a desirable solution, since its social cost is high and the increase in poverty would be real. The average replacement ratio of the Belgian welfare system is in no case higher than that of the welfare systems of neighbouring countries.

Another idea to consider for increasing the financial incentive to work is to augment the minima salaries. However, this proposal runs up against the fact that some low-productivity jobs are connected to labor costs that are too high (cf. the productivity trap). Furthermore, from an international perspective, the legal minimum wage in force in Belgium is relatively high, and such an action would run counter to the present policy of reducing the costs of low-production labor by lowering the employers' contributions.

A realistic proposal must be based on the principle that the gap between net income and welfare allowances can be enlarged without diminishing the welfare payment or increasing the total cost of labor. It is possible to reduce the tax and special tax pressures on salaries, which would result in a higher net salary without increasing the gross salary. Until now, the policy for lowering labor costs has essentially been limited to reducing the employer's contributions, so that only the cost of labor for the employer is reduced, without increasing the net salary of the worker or augmenting the financial incentive to work. So far, the effort has been focused on stimulating the demand for work. However, on the supply side, the negative implications of an excessive gap between the gross and the net salary also play a role. A relatively simple action in the area of the special tax, such as a reduction in the workers' social security contributions, could be the answer. For low-salary jobs, these contributions are far and away the largest factor in the gap between gross and net salary, and this measure could be gradually introduced according to the budgetary margin. The Belgian government has recently approved measures to reduce the workers' contributions for the lowest salaries, with a view to diminishing the unemployment traps.

Finally, it would be well to mitigate the sudden loss of certain complementary financial payments, such as increased family benefits. To this effect, the social partners formulated some proposals in their December 1999 report to the government.

Increasing financial incentives represents only one of the components of the strategy for limiting the risk of unemployment traps, if for no other reason than because of budgetary constraints. The structural interventions that bring about a change in perceptions by the workers as well as by the employers also play a decisive part. The problem of reaching an adequate level of training merits priority treatment. In this context, the importance of a solid basic training cannot be overstressed. In Belgium, the following elements are significant political challenges: increasing the number of persons with at least a diploma of higher secondary education, reassessing the technical and vocational teaching, and making a better adjustment between the young school leavers and the needs of society.

It would also be essential to increase the efforts in favor of life-long training. On this matter, the employers have equal responsibility. In the last inter-professional agreement, the social partners committed themselves to make additional efforts to supplement training programs. Finally, the job-seekers who are in danger of joining the long-term unemployed should be urged to follow a set of integration measures. The employment services should take an active part in these supplementary processes. More than a simple way of spending time usefully, this support should act as a solid and adequate bolster to the job-seekers' employability, with a job as its end result.

The employers' excessive requirements for qualification cause the less qualified to be excluded from the labor market by others who are more qualified and cause an under-utilization of the labor market potential. On the one hand, the relatively less-qualified persons are frightened by these excessive requirements and do not apply for certain jobs for which they could have been considered. On the other hand, the hiring of an over-qualified person in relation to the job requirements may lead to a loss of motivation and of qualification. A better adapted management of personnel is a possible solution to this.

While a combination of social benefits and complementary financial aids increases the risk of unemployment traps, this option responds to other political concerns, such as the fight against poverty.

In addition, there are other specific systems that also compound the financial unemployment traps, like the benefits favoring the aged unemployed or the mechanisms for automatic deductions from salaries.

Belgian unemployment insurance differs, however, from that of other western countries in its nearly unlimited duration for household heads, isolated persons and some cohabitants without family responsibilities, which could doubtless increase the probability of an unemployment trap. A specific approach designed to monitor the will to reintegrate would perhaps be helpful to this end.

Back to Work Allowance in Ireland

Tony Kieran

The Back to Work Allowance Scheme (BTWAS) was introduced in Ireland in 1993 as an active labor market measure targeted at the long-term unemployed. The central objectives of this measure are twofold:

- to enable the long-term unemployed to break the cycle of unemployment by taking up a job or becoming self-employed; and

- to permit the integration of the long-term unemployed into employment and self-employment.

This section outlines the background to the introduction of the BTWAS and sets the context in which the Back to Work Allowance Scheme was seen as a solution to some of the unemployment problems of the time. It will outline how the Scheme works and examine how successful it has been in meeting its objectives. Given the changing economic situation in Ireland in the intervening period, it will pose some questions as to the future role of this measure.

Background and Context

At the beginning of the 1990s, Ireland was experiencing a period of economic depression, with very high levels of unemployment and low levels of labor market participation. The unemployment rate in 1990 was 12.9 percent, despite the fact that large numbers of Irish people had emigrated during the years 1985 to 1990 in search of work elsewhere. The emigration levels are confirmed by the census of population statistics, which shows a decline in population between the years of 1986 and 1991 from 3,540,643 to 3,525,719. This population decline affected the younger sectors of the population in particular.

The unemployment rate at 12.9 percent hides another vital statistic. Statistics obtained from the Central Statistics Office (CSO) and the Labour Force Survey show that 8.3 percent of the workforce were long-term unemployed in 1990. The unemployment rate rose to 15.7 percent by 1993, with long-term unemployment reaching 9 percent around the same time.

Participation rates were low, with only 52.3 percent of the population active in 1992. Participation rates have increased steadily in the intervening period to reach an estimated rate of 58 percent in 1999. The significant change in this period has been in the rate of participation by women in the labor force. Only 36.2 percent of women participated in the workforce in 1992, but this figure had risen to 46 percent by 1999.

In 1987 the government and the social partners negotiated the first of a series of partnership agreements covering national wage increases and tax and social welfare improvements. Each of these agreements covers a three-year period, and the second one negotiated and agreed in 1990 set the context for this employment measure. The 1990 agreement entitled the *Program for Economic and Social Progress* (PESP) led to the setting up of local area partnerships around the country.

These partnerships were empowered to aid financially any unemployed person who had a worthwhile idea for creating his or her own employment. Unemployment was identified as one of the major problems facing the country at the time, so in return for moderate pay increases it was agreed to introduce some active labor market measures aimed at integrating the long-term unemployed into the workforce.

The introduction of the BTWAS addressed a weakness in the existing package of labor market measures. Prior to its introduction, the focus of labor market measures had been on temporary employment. Most of the labor market budget was spent on schemes such as the Community Employment Programme offering part-time temporary employment to the long-term unemployed. For example, in the year that the BTWAS was introduced, the number of participants on temporary employment programs for long-term unemployed is estimated to have been 21,000 and to have accounted for approximately 75 percent of FAS-aided provision for the adult unemployed.

How Does the BTWAS Work?

In effect, there are two different measures in existence. One is aimed at people returning to work with an employer, and the other is targeted at people creating their own self-employment. In essence, the Scheme allows the long-termed unemployed to retain their weekly social welfare payment for a period while working. There are some differences in the benefit retention, depending on whether the person is employed or self-employed.

Employed persons retain 75 percent of their weekly payment for the first year following their return to the labor force. This reduces to 50 percent for the second year, and 25 percent is retained for the third year following their return to work. They also retain "secondary benefits" such as medical aid, fuel allowance, back-to-school allowance and other aids appropriate to people who receive unemployment payments.

Self-employed persons retain their weekly benefits on a sliding scale for a four-year period following their return to work. One hundred percent is retained for the first year, 75 percent for the second, 50 percent for the third year and 25 percent for the final year of the Scheme. "Secondary benefits" are also retained, as in the case of people returning to direct employment. Self-employed participants can also benefit from a package of technical support measures. Typically, the technical supports available cover the provision of training for newly self-employed persons in skills associated with their work, or their obligations as self-employed persons under legislation (taxation, company returns, etc.). Expert advice can also be provided and paid for by way of technical assistance as required by the individual.

In order to qualify for the Scheme, a person must be aged 23 years or over and have been in receipt of (or have an underlying entitlement to) unemployment assistance for a minimum of 12 months. The duration criteria are interpreted flexibly (e.g., a total of two years unemployed over the previous three years with periods spent on labor market programs, such as the Community Employment Programme, being counted towards the minimum period of unemployment). Single parents in receipt of one-parent family benefit for a period of 12 months can also qualify for the Scheme.

As this measure is expected to aid job creation, as well as directing jobs towards the long-term unemployed, certain conditions apply to employers and jobs aided by the Scheme:

- The jobs they are seeking to fill must be new and not replace existing jobs.

- The jobs must have the potential to become permanent jobs. Short-term and temporary jobs are not eligible for support under the Scheme.

- The number of hours worked per week must be not less than 20.

An important feature of this measure is that it places the person in employment, as opposed to training or a temporary work scheme. The effect of this is that the individual gains valuable work experience and increases his/her employability even in the event of the job coming to an end.

Numbers and Spending on the BTWAS

By 1996 a total of 16,000 people were benefiting from this measure, and of this total 7,166 were directly employed, with the remaining 8,880 self-employed. The figures continued to rise to reach a total of 31,550 by December 1998. This figure breaks down to 14,500 employed participants and 17,050 self-employed participants. A further increase in numbers was experienced in 1999, with the total number of participants reaching 31,900 approximately by year end. The breakdown between employed and self-employed participants is similar to that in 1998, with the self-employed option continuing to be more popular. Statistics available from the Department of Social, Community and Family Affairs (DSCFA) show that a total of £102,767,000 was spent on this measure in 1998. This expenditure is rising fast and reached £122,437,000 for the year to the end of 1999.

In the context of the population and the number of people unemployed in Ireland, this continues to be an important labor market measure. The number of beneficiaries involved continues to grow, and the expenditure accounts for about two-thirds of the DSCFA expenditure on employment support measures. It should be noted that other government departments operate labor market supports, so this figure, while it is important, does not represent two-thirds of all labor market expenditure.

How successful has the BTWAS measure been in enticing the long-term unemployed to take up employment or self-employment?

This was one of the issues examined in a study carried out by WRC social and economic consultants on behalf of the Department of Social, Community and Family Affairs in 1997. The report entitled *Developing Active Welfare Policy* was published in October 1997 and examined among other things the circumstances of participants and their labor market behavior prior to entering the BTWAS. It also sought their views regarding what their circumstances would have been in the absence of the BTWAS.

The study found as follows:

- During the six months prior to becoming aware of the BTWAS over one-fourth (29 percent) of participants had not made a single job application and a further 19 percent had made between two and five. Thus, almost half (48 percent) of the intake to the BTWAS consisted of persons who had either not been actively seeking employment or who had made only limited efforts to get work.

- Among the long-term unemployed who had been active in the labor market prior to hearing about the BTWAS, a small proportion (18 percent) had obtained job offers. However, they did not take up these job offers because of the low wages and poor conditions associated with the job on offer. Thus, among the overall intake to the BTWAS there was a significant minority who had been experiencing an unemployment trap.

- Prior to entering the BTWAS just under two-thirds (62 percent) of participants had never participated in a labor market measure. The study concluded that the intake to the BTWAS catered for two main categories of participants: persons who had not been activated by other labor market programs, and those who, despite having previously participated in at least one labor market program, had not secured employment as a result of their participation.

On the basis of these findings, the study concluded that the BTWAS interacts with the situation of the long-term unemployed in two main ways. First, it activates those who have become discouraged. Second, in the case of the long-term unemployed who were seeking work but experiencing difficulties in securing suitable employment, it provides a link into employment and self-employment.

The study found that average wage rates among employees were low and that a high proportion of those who were self-employed had low incomes from their businesses, so the BTWAS and the payments associated with it were seen as playing an important role in getting the participant back to work.

These findings suggest that the BTWAS is playing a role in activating a substantial component of the long-term unemployed and that the central program mechanism is the financial incentive of being able to retain a component of welfare income.

To what extent has the BTWAS acted as an incentive for employers to offer jobs to the long-term unemployed?

This scheme is not primarily targeted towards employers. Potential employees are the primary focus, and it differs from other labor market measures in that the subsidy is paid to the employee. During the early years of the scheme's operation, employers benefited from a PRSI exemption scheme in respect of any employee who was in receipt of this payment. This had the effect of reducing the employer's overhead costs for two years following the commencement of employment and can be interpreted as a subsidy to the employer. Wage costs of employees involved in the scheme may in certain cases be lower than those of other employees, and this can also be interpreted as a subsidy to the employer.

WRC social and economic consultants examined the incentive effect on employers in their 1997 survey. Their study found that about one-third of employers only became aware of their new employees' entitlement to the BTWAS following recruitment. Thus, the allowance could not have acted as an incentive to these employers.

The survey also found that 47 percent of employers had reduced the wage paid for the work by a portion or by all of the employees' BTWAS. A further 10 percent of employers stated that they had specifically sought employees who qualified for the scheme.

Taken as a whole these figures suggest that the allowance acted as an incentive to 40 to 60 percent of employers to offer a job to the long-term unemployed.

How does the BTWAS perform when compared to other measures to assist the unemployed enter self-employment?

WRC social and economic consultants also studied this aspect of the measure in 1997. They concluded that survival rates on the program compared very favorably with those reported for other programs. The estimated three-year survival rate of 75 percent exceeds all other programs for which figures are available. Two major factors were identified as likely to be contributing to the high survival rate:

- The structure and duration of income support paid to self-employed participants: This is paid at a higher rate and for a longer duration than all other programs that were reviewed. The scheme is unique in providing income support at 100 percent of prior welfare income for a duration of one year. This has a substantial impact on the survival rate associated with this measure. If the first year is excluded when computing survival rates for the program (i.e., the survival rate at year three is considered to be the survival rate at year two), then the two-year survival rate for participants broadly corresponds to that found in the Danish and French programs. Even when computed on this basis, the two-year survival rate is higher than that found in relation to the UK Enterprise Allowance Scheme in operation at the same time.

- The positive impact of the economic environment prevailing over the period during which the survival rates were measured: The period 1993 to 1996 was one of persistently high rates of economic growth. This aspect will be dealt with in some detail later in this section.

The Irish Labor Market in the 1990s

It is important to consider the changes in the Irish labor market and in the Irish economy since the introduction of the BTWAS in evaluating the success and ongoing relevance of the measure. The figures show that there has been exceptional growth in the Irish economy since 1994 and that this growth continues to be sustained at a very high level, with GDP and GNP conservatively estimated to have increased by 7.9 percent and 6.8 percent respectively in 1999. Recovery in employment numbers has not been as rapid as that in output growth, but the number in employment reached almost 1.59 million in 1999 compared with 1.156 million in 1991, equivalent to an average annual rate of growth of 2.9 percent over the period. This figure is expected to reach 1.7 million in 2000.

Alongside this rapid growth in employment, unemployment has fallen sharply. According to survey-based estimates, the number of people out of work fell to 96,900 in the March-May period of 1999, compared with 199,000 in 1991 and a peak of 220,000 in 1993. The overall level of unemployment fell to just 5.7 percent of the labor force in March-May 1999 from a mid-1990s peak of 15.7 percent. The level continues to fall sharply, with an estimated 4.7 percent of the active population now unemployed.

In relation to the overall unemployed portion of the labor force, an important trend has been the substantial decline in the numbers of long-term unemployed. After rising to a peak of 128,200 in 1994, the number of long-term unemployed fell to 41,600 in the March-May period of 1999. This is equivalent to a long-term unemployment rate of 2.5 percent compared with 9.0 percent in 1994. As a proportion of total unemployment, the number of persons in long-term unemployment has fallen to 42.9 percent of the total in March-May 1999 from 63.9 percent in 1990. This is an important development, since it has been the long-term unemployed section of the labor force that has been the target of the BTWAS.

The rapid rate of growth in employment recorded since the early 1990s has been central to the substantial fall in unemployment in recent years. It has also helped to underpin the increase in the size of the labor force by encouraging higher rates of participation and inward migration. It is instructive to examine further the composition of employment creation since the early 1990s, so as to gain a greater understanding of the nature of the significant changes that have occurred in the Irish labor market.

Analysis of the figures shows that the manufacturing sector was the largest employer in 1998, accounting for 301,300 persons or 20 percent of the workforce. The high proportion of employment in manufacturing reflects the very fast average growth rate achieved in this sector since the early 1990s. Apart from manufacturing, the most important sectors are retail and wholesale (accounting for almost 14 percent in 1998), financial and other business services (11.1 percent), and education and health (14.2 percent). The figures indicate that employment in the agriculture, forestry and fishing sector had dropped to 136,000 in March-May 1999, while non-agricultural employment reached 1.46 million. Non-agricultural employment has experienced an average growth rate of 4.8 percent over the 1991-99 period. State-sponsored employment schemes (i.e., the Community Employment Scheme) saw a substantial increase from around 21,000 persons in 1993 to over 40,000 persons in 1995 and have remained stable at this level between 1995 and 1999. Public-sector employment growth has experienced very slow growth on average since the early 1990s and stood at 307,000 persons in March-May 1999, compared with 288,000 in 1991. Total private sector employment rose at an average annual rate of 6 percent, reaching a level of 1.1 million in 1999.

Predictions are that the economy will continue to experience growth over the coming years. Growth rates are expected to decline towards 4.5 percent by 2002 and to around 3.5 percent by the year 2010, as the period of rapid catch-up with the advanced economies experienced in recent years begins to taper off.

The outlook for employment expansion over the next five to seven years remains bright, with growth of above 3 percent expected between 1999 and 2001, after which the rate of job creation is likely to slow to between 1.5 percent and 2.7 percent per annum. Assuming that these growth rates materialize, the level of unemployment will continue to fall over the coming years.

Other Recent Trends

Recent economic prosperity has brought other changes to the Irish work environment. The Irish tax system has undergone substantial change since the early 1990s. Income tax was traditionally viewed as an inhibiting factor towards employment creation, but the tax take has reduced significantly over the past ten years. Tax-free allowances have doubled, and the standard rate of income tax has reduced from 30 percent in 1990-91 to 24 percent in 1999-2000. The marginal rates of 48 percent and 53 percent which operated in 1990-91 have been replaced by a single rate of 46 percent in 1999-2000. Income tax exemption limits for people with low incomes have also increased significantly over the period.

Pay related social insurance (PRSI) and other income levies have also reduced over the period. The employees' share of the PRSI contribution has reduced from 5.5 percent to 4.5 percent over the period 1990-99. Employers also pay a portion of the cost of PRSI. This rate has reduced marginally from 12.2 percent to 12.0 percent over the same period, but more significantly a reduced rate of 8.5 percent applicable to salaries of up to £14,560 per annum was introduced in the 1999-2000 budget. The net effect of these changes has been to reduce the cost to employers of employing people, while also ensuring that employees retain more of their wage when all deductions have been paid.

A minimum wage came into operation for the first time in April 2000. The introduction of this legislation and its operation should help deal with the problem of low wages on offer in certain sectors of the economy. This should help, in particular, the low-skilled long-term unemployed in their endeavours to get back into work with reasonable rates of pay.

Conclusions

Research has shown the BTWAS to be successful in enticing the long-term unemployed to take up employment and self-employment opportunities. In particular, the survival rate for self-employed start-ups is impressive. Research has also indicated that the rate of benefit retention plays an important role in the self-employed business survival rate.

The BTWAS has also served a useful role in directing work towards the long-term unemployed who had become most detached from the workforce. This is supported by research which confirmed that almost half (48 percent) of those going onto the scheme had not been engaged in any job-search activity prior to commencing on the scheme.

A further review of the measure is under way but has not been completed at the time of writing. This review is important, as it will cover the seven years of operation of the measure. It is likely that the findings will have an important bearing on the future shape and role of this measure.

Changes in the labor market and in legislation have helped address some of the problems which led to the introduction of the BTWAS. Long-term unemployment rates have reduced significantly over the period 1993 to 1999.

Taxation changes have contributed to a more favorable climate for job creation. The introduction of minimum wage legislation in 2000 should also help eliminate the problem of low pay as experienced in the low-skill sectors of the economy.

The ongoing need for this measure could be questioned in the current situation in Ireland. With low levels of unemployment and a trend towards earlier intervention in the unemployment cycle, a case could be made to abolish or modify the measure. However, unemployment traps continue to exist, and some problems relating to the interaction of the tax and welfare systems remain to be resolved. As a result, a significant number of long-term unemployed continue to be detached from the labor force and require some measure like the BTWAS to help them back to work. While the country has experienced unprecedented economic growth and job creation, different regions have benefited to differing degrees. Most of the growth in employment has occurred on the east coast, with the result that parts of the west continue to suffer high levels of unemployment. As a result, a case could be made for the future to have this measure applied on a regional basis, with differing criteria applied to different areas.

A significant number of long-term unemployed persons have been unemployed for very long periods. Consideration has been given to the introduction of a specially tailored version of the BTWAS to cater for these people. The scheme as envisaged would apply to very long-term unemployed persons (over five years unemployed and over 35 years old) and would incorporate features to take account of the specific needs of this group. One obvious need that has been identified with this group has been the retraining prior to commencing work.

In conclusion, it is accepted that the BTWAS has made a contribution to the long-term unemployed in their quest for work and their efforts to reintegrate into the labor force. It has played its part as one of a number of labor market measures available to the long-term unemployed. The changing economic situation in Ireland over the period has created many job opportunities, but this alone would not have addressed the needs of the long-term unemployed. The BTWAS is seen as having played an important role in enabling the long-term unemployed access to a share of these opportunities.

The Situation outside European Union Countries

Ross McKay, Ana Fotyga, Jaroslav Sumný, Mahrez Aït Belkacem

In most parts of the world, the employment situation remains unfavorable. Unemployment is thus a source of considerable worry in both industrialized and developing countries. The employability of workers is therefore increasingly an issue of concern. Evidence from a number of countries outside the European Union shows that active labor market measures are more and more targeted toward improving a job-seeker's employability. The emphasis is put on the size and quality of the workforce and, whenever possible, on active, tailor-made preventive measures for fighting unemployment and adapting workers to the challenges of the changing labor markets.

Obviously, the effectiveness of activation measures depends to a great extent upon a number of framework conditions in a given country and on the resources available to carry them through. As has been seen in the previous section and will become even more evident in the following section, improving employability is a complex and variable policy mix which needs to be adapted to each national situation. The priorities set in the countries in transition or in developing countries differ considerably from those in the highly industrialized countries. They primarily aim at improving economic conditions, investing in education, improving competitiveness and the functioning of the markets in goods, services and capital.

This section will focus on some policy measures implemented in four countries outside the European Union. These countries are New Zealand, Poland, Slovakia and Algeria. The selected examples are by no means exhaustive but are intended to demonstrate the impact and importance of measures put into action in countries other than the European Union.

The first of the four selected countries, New Zealand, represents an OECD country, while Poland and Slovakia reflect the present situation in countries of transition economies. Algeria is particularly interesting, since it is a country which quite recently (1994) implemented an unemployment scheme. Although lacking sufficient means, the unemployment insurance fund tried from the outset to focus on implementing active labor market measures with a view to making job-seekers employable.

New Zealand

Concerns about employability in New Zealand emerged following the economic restructuring of the late 1980s and early 1990s. Although the term employability is itself not much used in public debate about welfare and work but rather on the need for human capital investment to improve the skills and work-readiness of job-seekers, there is no doubt that behind it lie concerns about the employability of those receiving income support.

Generally speaking, it can be noted that with the most recent welfare reforms in New Zealand greater emphasis has been placed on the expectation that income support recipients will be available for work, including an expansion of the work requirement beyond the ranks of the unemployed, in particular to include lone parents. Furthermore, changes have been made to enhance the financial incentives for movement off benefit and into work by improving the returns to people from their work efforts, for example by the provision of in-work benefits for low-income earners.

Attention has also been paid to developing a range of different types of assistance to help beneficiaries to make the transition to work, including a range of employability measures, and changes have been made in the operational infrastructure to create a service delivery environment which is likely to give best effect to these changes. Various programs have been developed to address the issue of employability, which take different approaches to achieve the goal.

One such approach is aimed at enhancing the employability of job-seekers by upgrading their confidence and work skills through work experience placements. To that end, a range of programs has been established to meet this goal. The most significant is the Community Work Programme, established in October 1998 in conjunction with a restructuring of the main benefits for job-seekers. In this change, the former unemployment benefit, sickness benefit and training benefit were all replaced by the new Community Wage Programme. Provision was made for job-seekers to be required to participate in the associated Community Work Programme. The new Community Work Programme was designed as an enhanced version of a pre-existing program, known as the Community Task Force, which had been in operation since 1991 and was intended to be built up to cater for larger numbers of participants.

The program is aimed at building the confidence, work skills, motivation and self-esteem of job-seekers by providing them unpaid work experience opportunities. This also has benefits for communities. To participate in the program, an applicant must be designated as "long-term unemployed," i.e., unemployed for 26 weeks or more, or be considered to be at risk of becoming long-term unemployed. Community work placement may involve work of up to 20 hours per week, but not more than eight hours per day. Job-seekers may be required to participate in the program, although they may opt to participate voluntarily.

Participants continue to receive any benefit to which they may be entitled and may also be paid a non-taxable participation allowance of up to NZ$21 per week. They may also be reimbursed for actual and reasonable costs they incur in participating in the program, up to a further NZ$20 per week.

Community work opportunities may be sponsored by a range of organizations, such as voluntary agencies and work trusts, and are required to be of benefit to the community or the environment. In order to avoid displacement of other workers, sponsoring organizations are required to sign a declaration stating that the work would not be done by any other means if workers were not available under the program. Placements are also required to resemble a paid work environment as closely as possible. There is little available information, however, about the effectiveness of the scheme in enhancing the employability of job-seekers or improving their probability of subsequently finding employment.

In the year to 31 December 1999, 22,126 job-seekers participated in the Community Work Programme. To place this figure in context, 192,166 people who were classified as job-seekers were receiving the community wage at this date. More than half of all job-seekers exit from the community wage within 20 weeks, so that the target population for the program is likely to be considerably less than 100,000.

Another such program is the Work Experience Programme which offers short-term work experience placements in a workplace or work-type environment. Placements are between one and four weeks in duration, and the hours of participation must fall within the normal work hours of the business. Employers are selected to provide work experience placements on the basis that they can provide an opportunity for a participant to gain an overview of their business.

The Work Experience Programme incorporates two other pre-existing programs which were earlier operated as separate programs in their own right. The first of these, known as Job Link, was targeted at longer-term job-seekers, while the second, known as Job Intro, was targeted at young job-seekers. Both programs provided workplace experience and on-the-job-training for up to four weeks. Participants were not paid a wage or allowance, but continued to receive the unemployment benefit if they were eligible for it.

The Work Experience Programme operates on a small scale. In the year ending 31 December 1999, only 657 people had participated in the program. However, the numbers built up over the course of the year: three-quarters participated in the program in the latter half of the year. Most participants were longer-term job-seekers, who would have formally qualified for Job Link.

A small number of work experience placements is also available through the New Zealand Conservation Corps. In the year ending 31 December 1999, 266 people participated in such placements. Overall, during that year a total of 23,049 people participated in the

Work Experience Programme, the vast majority being Community Work Programme participants.

Poland and Slovakia: Employability in Transition Economies

With the inception of the process of transition to a market economy ten years ago, there was a rapid emergence of high unemployment right from the beginning of the transition process. In both Poland and Slovakia, unemployment rates rose dramatically, from 0 percent to above 15 percent, within two years of the initiation of the transition process.[23] A number of reforms have since then been implemented. Despite the many efforts undertaken over the past years, there is still continuing concern over the important numbers of unemployed, which has become recurrent and long term.

In both countries, unemployment insurance has implemented activation measures designed to improve the capacity of unemployed persons to enter or to return to the labor market, developing the potential of each through training programs, work experience, assistance in the search for a job or entrepreneurship. Clearly, the means vary according to the policy priorities set.

In *Poland*, for instance, training and education of the unemployed is considered a basic form of active labor market policy. It is seen as an effective and efficient tool to help attenuate the existing mismatch between supply and demand on the local labor markets. It avoids social exclusion and escaping unemployment because those trained do not drop out from the labor force resources, even if they do not find a job immediately.

Evidence shows that only 30 percent of the unemployed have secondary school or vocational education. After a one-month training course, the probability of finding a non-subsidized job increases substantially. However, almost 70 percent of all the unemployed have a low or very low level of education and are particularly exposed to long-term unemployment.

The activities conducted by the coordinating institutions and district and provincial labor offices are of great significance for the effectiveness of these programs. The education and training centres use modern methods of teaching and audio-visual equipment. They also propose practical activities which they present within companies.

One very important objective of the education and training programs is to support local enterprises by providing them with a qualified labor force which is capable of adapting immediately to the job. Positive results are achieved when cooperation between the employer and the unemployed is financially supported by the district labor office. In some instances, an education and training course is based on a tripartite agreement between the employer, the job-seeker and the labor office. In agreement with the employer, the participant is offered employment after completion of the course. Undoubtedly, this form of activation measure substantially improves the employability of the job-seeker. Table 5.3 shows the effectiveness of such education and training courses based on the tripartite agreement.

In brief, the effectiveness of the education and training program based on a tripartite agreement can be attributed to the following factors:

- the employer chooses the participant to attend a course;

- the employer has to comply with the provisions specified in the tripartite agreement;

- the participant has the possibility to acquire qualifications corresponding to the employer's needs.

Despite their success, these courses are for the time being still a marginal activity within the broad education and training program run by labor offices. The continuously changing labor market situation and uncertain conditions for running a business often build a reluctance towards making use of this measure.

Table 5.3
Effectiveness of Education and Training Courses,
Based on a Tripartite Agreement (1996-98)

Tripartite agreements Characteristic rates	Year		
	1996	**1997**	**1998**
Number of schooled persons	4336	5646	6516
Number of employed persons	3630	4782	5137
Rate of employability	83.7 %	84.7 %	87.6 %

Source: *Labour Market*, no. 11, Nov. 1999.

It should be added that the financial means assigned by the labor funds to the education and training of the unemployed are, despite a considerable increase, still a symbolic value. The rate of re-employment, after the breakdown in 1997, exceeded 50 percent the year after. A more dynamic development of this active labor market measure geared to improve the employability of the job-seeker is expected upon Poland's anticipated entry to the European Union.

In *Slovakia,* the labor market is equally characterized by a high mismatch between supply and demand on the labor market. The unemployment level is 19 to 20 percent. The share of long-term unemployed is nearly 50 percent, and the average time of registered unemployment exceeds 15 months.

Since 1995, one important policy measure has been the creation of small and medium-sized enterprises (SMEs). The main objective of the creation of SMEs is to get the long-term unemployed as well as those in danger of becoming long-term unemployed off benefits. To that end, a program was set up under the umbrella of a non-profit society, CEPAC SLOVAKIA. It was founded by the National Labour Office, the National Agency for the Development of Small and Medium-sized Enterprises and CEPAC Soissons, a French partner.

A training and counselling program was developed which coaches training graduates while they are setting up their own business and monitors and counsels them after the establishment of a business.

The mission and tasks of the program are the following:

- to train future entrepreneurs chosen from among the registered unemployed or from among those identified as being in danger of losing their jobs;

- to improve the professional capacity of lecturers and counsellors who are designated to train the program's participants;

- to monitor and maintain contacts and cooperation with the program's graduates;

- to apply the CEPAC philosophy, which is geared to enable people who have lost employment to find their place in the labor market.

The program consists of four stages:

| Selection | | Training | | Coaching | | Monitoring |

Set up a business

Attendance in the program is based on a series of selection criteria such as a qualifications and work experience, entrepreneurial ideas, business sense, family background, personal characteristics, and access to funds.

The training part of the program includes theoretical as well as practical preparation in marketing, law, financial management, tax issues, bookkeeping, etc. At this stage, the participant is already developing a plan of how to set up a business.

Coaching represents the stage prior to and monitoring the stage following the establishment of the participant's own business. The aim is to provide the participant counselling and consultation in order to enable optimal preparation and a good start in his/her entrepreneurial activities. At the end of the course, the participant has to present the final project of the planned business and is required to defend it before a special commission. If this is accomplished successfully, the graduate will receive a diploma.

The training and counselling program is carried out in training centres which have been established throughout the country. There are approximately 30 to 40 courses held per year and about 500 to 600 participants in total per year. A breakdown by age reveals that the highest number of participants comes from the age group of 36-50 (35-40 percent), followed by the age group of 26-35 (30-35 percent) and then those under 25 (25-28 percent). To date, the program has helped almost 1,300 persons to find a job. New SMEs are mainly established in the service sector (55 to 60 percent) followed by trade, which accounts for 15 to 20 percent. An evaluation of the program is carried out in order to improve services.

Algeria

The Algerian unemployment scheme is very recent. It was legally constituted in 1994 but has only been effectively functioning since September 1996.

Unemployment in Algeria is above all characterized by a very high proportion of first-time job-seekers. Official figures quote unemployment at 29.5 percent of the working population, with around

2 million unemployed in an active population of 8 million of working age out of a total population of 30 million.

Apart from paying a replacement income, i.e., passive labor market measures, to the unemployed, the unemployment benefit scheme includes provision for sustaining the jobs of beneficiaries who are in work, encouraging beneficiaries to go back to work, prioritizing training schemes aimed at facilitating the return to work and participating in activities aimed at preventing unemployment. From the outset, the Algerian unemployment fund (CNAC) saw the implementation of labor market measures geared to improve the employability of the job-seekers as an essential tool, although the financial means at the CNAC's disposal have been very restricted.

Specific surveys carried out on unemployment beneficiaries revealed that about half of the unemployed are without any particular qualification and in most cases illiterate. Their chance of finding a job without assistance is rather doubtful, bearing the present labor market situation in mind. They can only be employable when becoming literate and having acquired basic skills.

Whilst the CNAC is aware that the battle against illiteracy is the responsibility of the government, the fact remains that the sheer numbers of illiterate unemployed considerably discourage action by the fund, which is pessimistic regarding the job chances of the beneficiaries in question. However, the CNAC is playing an essential part in improving the employment situation of its clients by implementing very specific tailor-made measures.

Hence, the CNAC took the initiative to carry out a pilot project in two regions, which it is hoped will be expanded to other regions of the country. The project consists of two phases:

- the first phase encompasses a four-month literacy course offered to illiterate job-seekers;

- the second phase concentrates on training in basic subjects and skills.

It is hoped that this project will prove its relevance and that the government will perceive the need to commit funds for this purpose with a view to responding to the problem of unemployment and to equip job-seekers with some basic skills.

Notes

1.   Employment Service, *New Deal: Objectives, monitoring, evaluation*, Sheffield, UK, 1997.
2.   C. Hasluck, "The New Deal for Young People, two years on," *Research and Development Report*, The Employment Service, forthcoming, 2000.
3.   In October 1996, JSA replaced the previous systems of unemployment benefit and income support.
4.   Groups eligible for early entry to the NDYP include people with disabilities, ex-offenders, those leaving local authority residential care, and individuals with literacy or numeracy problems.
5.   Note that options 1, 2, and 3 all include at least one day a week of training towards a recognized vocational qualification.
6.   The eligibility criterion is relaxed to one year or more for members of certain disadvantaged groups.
7.   Hasluck, op. cit.
8.   House of Commons, *The New Deal pathfinders*, House of Commons Education and Employment Committee, Session 1997-98, London, UK, The Stationery Office, Aug. 1998.
9.   ibid, p. 62.
10.   Hasluck, 2000 reports that over 90 percent of those leaving the employment option directly enter an unsubsidized job, compared with only around 60 percent of those leaving the New Deal from the other three main options.
11.   On the selection effect, Hasluck, 2000 reports monitoring evidence showing that certain disadvantaged groups are under-represented on the employment option, e.g., participants with disabilities and those from ethnic minority groups, and that multiply disadvantaged participants are over-represented on the full-time education and training option and the environmental task force options, in particular.
12.   N. Meager; C. Evans, "The evaluation of active labour market measures for the long-term unemployed," *Employment and Training Papers No. 16*, International Labour Office, Geneva, 1998.
13.   It is notable that previous experiments in the United Kingdom which linked scheme non-participation with benefit sanctions, notably the Project Work Pilots for the long-term unemployed, also recorded high "disappearance rates." See the discussion of this in Employment Service, 1997.
14.   B. Anderton, R. Riley, G. Young, "The New Deal for Young People: First year analysis of implications for the macroeconomy," *Research and Development Report ESR33*, The Employment Service, Sheffield, UK, Dec. 1999.
15.   R. Legard, D. Molloy, J. Ritchie, T. Saunders, "New Deal for Long-Term Unemployed People: Qualitative work with individuals, stage one," *Research and Development Report ESR38*, The Employment Service, Sheffield, UK, Jan. 2000; Tavistock Institute, "Case study evaluation of the New Deal for the Long-Term Unemployed: National provision for those aged 25 and over: A review of progress in five units of delivery, *Research and Development Report ESR31*, Sheffield, UK, Nov. 1999; J. Atkinson, J. Barry, J. Blanden, S. Dewson, K. Walsh, "Case studies to evaluate the NDLTU November pilots, *Research and Development Report*, the Employment Service, Sheffield, UK, forthcoming, 2000.
16.   L. Delsen; J. Visser, "Flexibilisering van de arbeid via CAO's" (Flexibilization of labour through collective agreements), in *SMA*, June 1999, no. 6, pp. 296-305.
17.   J.G.L. Thijssen, "Employability in het brandpunt" (Employability in focus), in *Tijdschrift voor HRM*, 1, 2000, pp. 7-34.

18.   J.G.L. Thijssen, "Historie, concepten en scenarios" (History, concepts and scenarios), in M. Baarveld, P. Bakker, J. van Erp, J. Gasperz, R. Kip, P. Lapperre, J. Thijssen, *Employability. Bewegen in vogelvlucht, Stichting Maatschappij en Onderneming*, 1999.
19.   Labor Accounts, CBS-Statistics Netherlands.
20.   "Schoolverlaters tussen onderwijs en arbeidsmarkt 1998"(School leavers between education and labor market), *ROA*, 1999/5.
21.   B. de Lange, M. Thunnissen, "De arbeidsmarkt als stuwraket: van flexibilisering van de arbeid naar employability" (The labor market as propelling force: From flexibility of labor to employability), *Bijdrage aan de Nederlandse Arbeidsmarktdag 2000*, IVA, Tilburg, 2000.
22.   OSA labor supply panel data.
23.   ILO, *Report V*, International Labour Conference, 83rd Session, 1996, "Employment policies in a global context."

Part 3

Trends

6

Moving from Unemployment to Employment Insurance: The Case of Canada

Nancy Fedorovitch

In 1996-97, Canada implemented a new Employment Insurance Act, replacing the former Unemployment Insurance Act. The change in name was significant, as the Canadian government wished to change the focus of workers from "How can I qualify for benefits?" to "How can I obtain more work, stay employed and have a brighter future?"

Over the years, administrators had noticed that in some cases some people had become dependent upon unemployment benefits. It was discovered that in 1991, in fact, 38 percent of claimants had established three or more claims within five years, and 50 percent of claimants had established two or more claims within a five-year period.[1]

"Unemployment insurance had become an annual income supplementation system, not an insurance programme."[2] In surveys conducted with employers, it was reported that in parts of the country where average wages are low employers were unable to hire workers once those workers began a claim for unemployment insurance benefits. Some employers stated that their biggest competition for workers was, in fact, the unemployment insurance system.[3] Meanwhile, the unemployment insurance account had often been in deficit, and there was increasing structural unemployment as companies downsized and adjusted to modern global markets.

An extensive study of the Canadian labor market and the problems of workers set the foundation for the employment insurance reform. Such studies concluded that "too many employable adults face chronic unemployment...too many of our youth find it difficult to make the transition from school to work."[4] It was also noted that government spending on social programs was outpacing economic growth. There were growing concerns "about how well the programmes work...to address the real problems faced by employable adults."[5]

While both the Unemployment Insurance Act and the current Employment Insurance Act are meant to provide temporary income support to those who have become unemployed through no fault of their own, the new Employment Insurance Act shifted the perspective to prevention of repeat usage through a number of measures that discouraged claims for benefit, while encouraging employment. Furthermore, there was a new thrust for individuals to take more responsibility for acting as partners in that effort.

The new legislation therefore had a rationale which significantly departed from that of its predecessor. The intention was to persuade people away from dependency behavior and to encourage them to think in terms of prevention of unemployment. The new Employment Insurance Act encouraged greater workforce attachment, reduced benefit levels for frequent claimants, and encouraged active re-employment measures rather than passive income support. Cost savings from the lower employment insurance benefit payout were to be diverted into funding more positive solutions.

Support measures were introduced to help organizations provide services such as job-finding clubs or group job counseling to assist those with barriers to employment. In addition, there are targeted wage subsidies, self-employment assistance to help people start a business, targeted earnings supplements, and job-creation partnerships to help people acquire job experience.

Before moving on to the specifics of the active support measures, it will be useful to examine the features of the Employment Insurance Act which are intended to move the focus of claimants toward their own employability and away from reliance upon unemployment insurance.

Employment Insurance Features

A key feature of the new Employment Insurance Act is that it is an *hours-based* system. This is part of the new employment insurance focus on employment. The hours system provides a clearer link between work and benefits. Previously, individuals acquired *weeks* of insured employment in order to qualify for benefits. That meant that whether a person worked 15 hours or 70 hours in a week, he or she would be given credit for only *one* insured week.

By changing to an hours-based system, a person is given credit for each hour worked, i.e., a person working 70 hours per week for ten weeks would receive credit for 700 hours, which is considered to be the equivalent of 20 weeks of work at 35 hours per week. Working long hours with high earnings in a short ten-week period would also tend to raise the benefit rate if the earnings happened to fall into the period used to calculate the rate of benefit.

Under the new system, each hour and each dollar are counted. Previously, those working less than 15 hours per week were not covered by unemployment insurance, and premiums did not have to be paid. This led in some circumstances to employers restricting the amount of work available to an employee. In addition, some employees adjusted their work effort only to have the minimum of 15 hours in any week. There is no longer any particular advantage to hiring people for a minimum of hours, and individuals do not acquire an insured week by working as little as possible. At the same time, those who are only marginally attached to the labor force, i.e., whose insured earnings are only Can$2,000 or less, receive a refund of their premiums.

The number of hours required in order to qualify for benefits depends upon the economic region in which the claimant resides. The claimant needs from 420 to 700 hours to qualify. In areas of high unemployment, fewer hours are required to qualify for benefits than, for example, in booming economic regions that have a very low unemployment rate. Moreover, claim duration would be longer in the areas where the economy is not robust. There are currently 54 economic regions.

The net result is to encourage those living in low unemployment areas/high opportunity areas to work longer in order to qualify. Since the claim duration is also shortened in areas of high opportunity, the shorter claim is meant to encourage the unemployed to obtain a job as soon as possible. Of course, the legislation has always stipulated that claimants must prove their availability for work and must be able to prove a reasonable job-search effort.

A new entrant or a re-entrant to the labor force has higher qualifying conditions. If such a person has a limited labor force attachment over a two-year period, then he or she will require 910 insured hours to qualify no matter how economically depressed the community may be. The design rationale was that dependency should not be fostered when a person enters the labor market.

Special benefits, made up of maternity, parental and sickness benefits, have a fixed entrance requirement of 700 hours for the whole country.[6]

The Employment Insurance Act contains measures that focus on frequent claimants. When a claimant files for benefits, the previous five years are examined to determine whether the claimant has had any previous claims in that period. If so, the benefit rate, currently at 55 percent, is reduced by 1 percent for every 20 weeks of benefits claimed. However, the lowest benefit rate is 50 percent of the insured earnings of that claimant. This is referred to as "the intensity rule."

Another measure which targets repeat usage is "the clawback provision" focusing on higher- income repeat users. Those with a net income of Can$39,000 or more who have claimed benefits during a taxation year and have claimed 20 weeks or more of benefits in the past five years have to repay employment insurance benefits based on the intensity of usage. Again, this provision is meant to discourage high-income individuals from relying upon benefits.

On the other hand, claimants are encouraged to accept work while on claim, as they are allowed to earn 25 percent of their benefit rate or Can$50, whichever is higher, before the earnings are deducted from their weekly benefits. Very stringent provisions exist regarding undeclared earnings, including penalties, higher entrance requirements on subsequent claims, and even prosecution.

Employability and the Employment Benefits and Support Measures

The rest of this chapter will discuss this new focus on employability. While most of the Employment Insurance Act pertains in some way to benefits payable to the unemployed, the qualifying and entitlement conditions, premiums, etc., Part II of the Act provides the legislation related to employment benefits and the national employment service. At the outset, the legislation takes a novel approach in that it first establishes the underlying policy of the legislation, rather than simply outlining a number of rules and entitlements.

The legislation, in fact, explicitly states that employment benefits and support measures are to be established in accordance with the following guidelines. The employment benefits and support measures must:

- harmonize with provincial employment measures and avoid duplication;

- reduce dependency on unemployment benefits by helping individuals obtain or keep employment;

- create cooperation and partnership with other governments, employers, and community-based organizations;

- be flexible and entail local decision-making;

- be available in both official languages;

- commit persons receiving assistance to achieving the goals of the assistance and to take primary responsibility for identifying their needs and locating services to meet those needs and to share the cost of the assistance;

- be evaluated to determine their success in assisting persons to obtain or keep employment.[7]

Persons eligible for employment assistance benefits are those who are unemployed and for whom a benefit period for employment insurance benefits is established or whose benefit period ran out 36 months ago. The look-back window is 60 months for those who had received benefits for maternity, adoption and/or parental benefits and who are now wishing to re-enter the labor force. This is set down in the legislation.[8]

In order to avoid duplication of effort at the federal and provincial levels and to ensure that programming is more responsive to local labor market realities, the federal government has entered into federal-provincial labor market agreements. Certain responsibilities in employability would be assumed at the provincial level or co-managed by both levels of government and funded through the employment insurance account. For example, since education is a provincial jurisdiction, it was a logical progression for the federal government to gradually withdraw from labor market training, apprenticeship programs and other workplace-based training. The federal-provincial labor market agreements are ongoing and are to be reassessed every three years.

The parties to the agreements together set annual targets, including returns to work, savings to the employment insurance account and priority access for employment insurance claimants.

The federal government, however, continues to be responsible for overall management of the employment insurance account and delivery of employment insurance benefits. The federal government also continues to provide services commonly referred to as being pan-Canadian. This would include national emergency measures, inter-provincial worker mobility, national labor market information, national partnerships with labor market sectors, national labor exchange systems, and pilot projects to explore a variety of approaches.

In order to implement employment benefits and support measures, the federal Government may provide financial assistance in the form of grants and contributions, loans or loan guarantees. Insurance benefits and contributions are the tools used the most often.

The legislation also makes provisions for penalties in the event of fraud. The employment insurance legislation in general has a low tolerance for fraud, and therefore Part II related to employment benefits and support measures is no exception.

The foregoing portion of this chapter provides a very brief summary of the recent legislative changes, as well as the underlying rationale for those changes.

How Have the Reforms to the Employment Insurance Income Benefits Fared?

In 1998, 80 percent of Canadians who were laid off or quit with just cause were eligible to receive benefits. However, employment insurance does not insure all perils nor address every problem a worker may encounter. It was never meant to cover people who had:

- never worked and never contributed to employment insurance;

- decided to return to work after a long absence;

- been self-employed and did not contribute to employment insurance;

- quit for no valid reason or been fired for misconduct.

Between 1995-96 and 1997-98, total claims fell by 14 percent, and benefit payout declined by Can$2 billion. In 1998-99, the total number of claims was about the same, but the benefit payout was higher.

The reform has, however, coincided with a strong resurgence in the economy. The unemployment rate has dropped in this period from 9.6 percent to 6.8 percent, which is the lowest level in over a decade. Wages have begun to rise again, as well.

Moreover, premiums have been lowered from Can$3.07 in 1994 to Can$2.40 for year 2000. The surplus has also grown to healthy levels and will cushion the effect of any recession, should one occur.[9]

How Have the Active Measures Fared?
(employability measures)

In 1997-98, employment insurance provided 482,000 EBSMs (employment benefits and support measures) interventions to clients. These included longer-term interventions such as training purchases and self-employment assistance and shorter-term interventions such as employment assistance services, counselling and group services. During the same period, some Can$2 billion was spent on EBSMs, including Can$465 million on income benefits to employment insurance clients participating in EBSMs. In 1998-99, there was a shift to more short-term interventions; however, the use of targeted wage subsidies doubled in 1998-99. The average cost of interventions decreased.[10]

For 1997-98, the number of clients receiving EBSMs who returned to work was 183,000 compared to a target of 174,000. This resulted in potential unpaid benefits of Can$674 million. For 1998-99, 267,108 clients returned to work, and unpaid benefits totalled Can$917.

The Transitional Jobs Fund ended on 31 March 1999. It created 30,000 jobs. Under the new Canada Jobs Fund (CJF), the creation of sustainable jobs will continue, as the objective of the CJF is to create long-term sustainable jobs for individuals in high unemployment areas and to strengthen the capacity of communities to become self-reliant. This objective will be achieved by working in collaboration with partners such as the provinces/territories, regional economic development agencies, other federal government departments, community partners and the private sector in a manner that respects local and regional priorities.

Labor Market Programs Outside Employment Insurance

Employment insurance was never intended to have all the answers, nor all of the solutions. Nonetheless, employability is an issue at the heart of the core values of Human Resources Development Canada (HRDC). Moreover, HRDC is working with other Canadian federal departments in strategies that work in concert with employment insurance and its active measures.

HRDC's Human Resources Investment Branch helps the government of Canada promote its agendas related to employment, youth, learning and literacy. The Human Resources Investment Branch also brings together various levels of government, employers, sector councils, workers and educators in an effort to address issues that ultimately impact upon employability of Canadians. Moreover, since Part II of the Employment Insurance Act addresses only those Canadians who are eligible for employment insurance or who have been in receipt of employment insurance within a 36- to 60-month window, the Human Resources Investment Branch reaches out to other Canadians who have no fewer needs in adapting to an ever-changing and ever-challenging Canadian labor market.

The following outlines the many varied programs administered through the Human Resources Investment Branch. Only a brief description of these programs is provided, as space limitations dictate only an introduction to these many initiatives. It should be borne in mind that extensive information is available on the HRDC website: *www.hrdc-drhc.gc.ca*, and more particularly in the publication on the website, *Guide to Human Resources Development Canada*. The following information is, in fact, extracted from that publication and not devised by this author.

The Youth Employment Strategy

There are many facets to this strategy, too extensive to be covered here. However, one publication that does seek to summarize such an extensive initiative is, in fact, given to youth to enable them to access relevant information. Under HRDC's Youth Employment Strategy, young people have been given information in a publication called *Youth Link 1999-2000*. This publication contains information on the following:

Financial help to obtain an education

Awards, bursaries, fellowships, grants and scholarships are enumerated. These come largely from the private sector. In addition, there is information on how to access the Canada Education Savings Grant and the Canada Student Loans Programme.

The Canada Student Loans Programme provides up to Can$165 per week of study to eligible post-secondary students. Loans are negotiated through the Canadian banks and credit unions. The Canadian Education Savings Grant is a program to help parents, grandparents and interested Canadians to save for a child's post-secondary education by paying grants of up to Can$400 per year to beneficiaries of registered education savings plans. The grants top up the savings in the plans.

Career information tools

The book also provides an index of further information on various interfaces with potential employers or contacts such as information on career week, sector councils, the labor market information website (*http://lmi-imt.hrdc-drhc.gc.ca*).

Entrepreneurship

For those wishing to become self-employed, resources such as the Business Development Bank of Canada and other financing sources are mentioned.

Job search

Listed are the Canada WorkinfoNET (*http://www.workinfonet.ca*); the Electronic Labour Exchange (*http://www.ele-spe.org*), the Job Bank (*http://jb-ge.hrdc-drhc.gc.ca*); Work Search (*http://www.worksearch.gc.ca*) and others.

Skills development and learning opportunities

Various organizations are listed to help youth access this information. Examples are references to the Aboriginal Friendship Centre Programme and Peer Helper Programmes for Out-of-the-Mainstream Youth.

Work/travel/international opportunities

Mention is made of various working holiday programs and student exchange programs, the Youth International Internship Programme, Canadian Crossroads International and many others.

Youth Internship Canada

This program provides funding to employers who create meaningful work experiences for unemployed and under-employed youth.

The emphasis is on science and technology and international trade and development.

Youth Service Canada

This program provides funding to organizations which create community service projects for youth who face greater barriers to entering the labor market.

Other Employment Support Measures

Employment assistance services

A range of services is provided, including help on preparing resumés, job-finding clubs, counseling or individual or group employment sessions.

Local labor market partnerships

Partnerships with local governments, communities, workers, employers and various labor and other agencies have been formed to help improve prospects for both the unemployed and those who may likely become unemployed.

Sectoral partnerships initiative

The following key objectives are enumerated on the HRDC website. The sector partnerships are to:

1.   develop effective partnerships in and with the private sector,

2.   improve the relevance of the learning system,

3.   foster a lifelong learning culture within industry,

4.   support the mobility of labor across Canada, and

5.   contribute to Canada's labor market information.

Canada Jobs Fund

The objective of this fund is to create long-term sustainable jobs in high unemployment areas and to build self-reliant communities. Approval for all CJF proposals rests with the Minister of HRDC. Eligible sponsors include businesses, organizations, individuals, municipal governments and band/tribal councils.

Employability assistance for people with disabilities

The Government of Canada shares half of the costs (up to a maximum) with the provinces for a comprehensive range of measures to help the disabled prepare for, obtain and retain employment.

Opportunities Fund Program

This program assists 4,000 to 6,000 disabled persons per year to prepare for, obtain and retain employment. This is a Can$30-million-per-year project for those who are not employment insurance eligible. This program terminated on 31 March 2000.

Older workers' pilot projects

Older workers who have been displaced due to structural unemployment and who have low literacy skills are particularly problematic. Many general programs aimed at improving the employability of clients do not work for older workers. Instead, a more targeted approach is required. Older workers tend to have a lower educational level and to have been employed in declining industries. Moreover, they are often reluctant to relocate or undergo training programs.

In order to learn what may work, a joint federal-provincial-territorial working group was formed to chronicle what is known, what worked in the past to encourage re-employment, and to run pilot projects designed and delivered in the provinces and territories. The federal government is providing Can$30 million for the pilots. Afterward, there will be an evaluation of what worked and what could be done nationally in the light of lessons learned.

Learning and Literacy Directorate

This HRDC Directorate within the Human Resources Investment Branch promotes lifelong learning. The focus is on financial assistance to post-secondary students, access to international education, utilization of learning technologies and increasing awareness of the importance of literacy.

Aboriginal human resources development strategy

This Can$1.6 billion five-year initiative came into effect in April 1999. Aboriginal organizations are to deliver labor market programs, as well as programs for youth, persons with disabilities, and child care for First Nations and Inuit. Part of this program is an urban program with Can$30 million a year aimed at delivering programs and services to Aboriginal people living in urban areas or off-reserve.

Conclusions

The programs and services aimed at improving the employability of Canadians have gone well beyond the limitations of the legislation to pay benefits to the unemployed. While Part II of the Employment Insurance Act contains many important collaborative strategies aimed at federal-provincial cooperation in improving the employability of Canadians, there are Canadians who are not eligible for the employment insurance scheme and have not paid employment insurance premiums. These Canadians are being helped as part of an overall prevention strategy to encourage workforce attachment, encourage literacy and lifelong learning, and adapt to changing labor markets.

The lessons learned from all of these initiatives are many, but, in general, it has been confirmed that targeting can make a difference, and tailoring programs and initiatives not just to a particular local labor market or group but also to the individual can make the difference between success and disappointment. People of different educational levels, different backgrounds, skills, experiences and in different stages of life have different needs which must be taken into account.

The best way to achieve results is also to recognize the value of partnerships. Each level of government, workers, employers and various groups have important contributions to make in meeting challenges of particular communities, groups, industries and individuals. They all bring their experience, skills and talents to projects. No longer can programs, projects and funding be offered in isolation, without regard to the complex labor market, economic, and sociocultural contexts.

While in the past programs and policies were geared to immediate problems, the new focus is on prevention. The time horizon in some cases is much longer, and it can be less rewarding to work toward goals that do not show immediate payoffs. Evaluations are planned of the results of the different federal-provincial-territorial labor market agreements. These will be important in understanding the impact of these measures on individuals returning to work. Evaluations are also being conducted on the various grants programs mentioned above. Attention has focused recently on the efficacy of some of these programs.

As Canada's unemployment rate continues to decline to historically low levels, more job opportunities are available. Employers may become less demanding when looking for new employees, and lower-skilled employees may have a better chance of finding employment. In this situation, the emphasis shifts from providing temporary income support to increasing the labor market.

Nonetheless, the problems of seasonality of work and repeat usage of the employment insurance fund continue. The issue is once again under study. In some cases, it is not a question of the employability of the employment insurance recipients; rather, it is more a question of employment opportunities in the off-season. Still there are those who have been reluctant to take other jobs, preferring instead to wait to return to the traditional seasonal employer. The government emphasis remains on community capacity building, rather than returning to a policy of dependence on benefits.

While the debate continues, there is one certainty: Canada's place in the global market cannot be achieved by dependency, but rather by an educated knowledge-based workforce with employable skills that are in demand.

The employment insurance legislation is subject to a five-year requirement to monitor and report to Parliament. In addition, there will be increased activity in evaluating results of the various grants programs and the individual projects funded.

HRDC is committed to helping Canadians find and keep employment and to helping them when they temporarily lose their jobs. The changing labor market presents additional challenges. As the Government of Canada stated in its last Speech from the Throne:

> The Government will forge partnerships with other governments, public- and private-sector organizations, and Canadian men and women to establish a national action plan on skills and learning for the twenty-first century. This plan will focus on lifelong learning, address the challenge of poor literacy among adults, and provide citizens with the information they need to make good decisions about developing their skills.[11]

Notes

1. *Improving social security in Canada: From unemployment insurance to employment insurance*, a supplementary paper, Human Resources Development Canada (HRDC), 1994, p.15.
2. Ibid., p. 16.
3. *Jobs with a future*, Report of the Working Group on Seasonal Work and Unemployment Insurance, HRDC, March 1995, p. 41.
4. *Social security in Canada: Background facts*, HRDC, February 1994, p. 44.
5. Ibid., p. 44.
6. New draft legislation is contemplating lowering the entrance requirements for special benefits to 600 hours.
7. Section 57, Employment Insurance Act, Part II.
8. Idem, section 58.
9. All data from the HRDC Monitoring and Assessment Reports for the fiscal years stated.
10. Ibid.
11. Speech from the Throne, 12 October 1999.

7

Outlook

Recognition and Stabilization of the Notion of Employability

The notion of employability, which has been the object of widely differing interpretations since its appearance at the beginning of the twentieth century, is defined in its *current version* as the relative capacity of an individual for obtaining employment with account being taken of the interaction between his/her personal characteristics and the labor market. The main operational consequences are therefore the mobilization of employment policies with the promotion of multidimensional and negotiated approaches.

Promotion of employability consists mainly of developing what are called active measures furthering adaptation to the labor market, as a supplement to income-assistance measures for persons deprived of employment, in a preventive and individualized manner if possible.

The development of employability measures, the forms and contents of which vary according to the constraints and particularities of each state but which represent a general trend, has been given impetus particularly by the European Employment Strategy and by the example of certain national, European and extra-community models.

The Impetus of the European Commission...

The European Commission, through several guidelines, has accordingly assigned to the member states objectives for the development of employability. States must, in the first instance, offer to every young person, before he/she reaches six months of unemployment, and to unemployed adults, before 12 months of unemployment, a "new start" in the form of measures intended to facilitate access or a return to the labor market (training, work experience, individual close support in counseling, etc.). States must then extend the number of beneficiaries of active measures to at least 20 percent of the unemployed.

Each state must also examine and, if need be, redirect its compensation and tax systems, so as to encourage unemployed or inactive persons to look for and seize employment possibilities or to strengthen their capacity for entry into working life and for employers to create new jobs.

Finally, states must finalize a policy aimed at prolonging the active life of older workers by making possible the maintenance of capacity for work, lifelong learning or other flexible working formulae.

The implementation of the European strategy by states progressively traces the lines of *a European social model* based on the integration of social protection systems and mechanisms furthering the development of employment.

... And the Examples Provided by Certain National Models

European thinking and the direction being taken, pursued by states, have themselves often been inspired by national models. Examples of measures and practices which satisfy the objectives set by the Commission are therefore to be found throughout the various systems.

Many states have thus put in place programs intended to promote the entry or the reassignment of categories of job-seekers the most removed from the labor market. This is the case of the New Deal for Young People in the United Kingdom, which offers a program requiring young persons without work, aged from 18 to 24, to choose, after a prerequisite period of guidance for a maximum of four months, among various options combining training and occupational experience. If the job-seeker refuses to choose one of these options, his/her unemployment benefits are suspended for two to four weeks. The New Deal therefore constitutes not only a measure of activation of the labor market, in the traditional sense, but also a key element in the British government's *welfare to work* strategy.

The will to do away with brakes on activity leads to wondering as well about the factors playing a role in the decision of an unemployed person to accept or refuse a job and in the choice of favoring a situation of dependence on benefits rather than working. Among the *unemployment traps* is the financial trap, when obtaining work does not result, or results very little, in an increase in purchasing power. It is evident, for example, from the research carried out in Belgium that the minimum increase in income must be of at least 15 percent in order for job-seekers to accept.

Policies intended to eliminate these traps, set in particular for persons with weak qualifications who cannot aspire to the best-paid jobs, must therefore incorporate provisions which create genuine financial incentives for resuming work. However, the solutions cannot be limited either to a systematic increase in the cost of labor, which would risk reducing job offers, or to excessively lowering benefits with the attendant high social risk. Other possibilities have been put forward such as, for example, a reduction of the social contributions of workers which constitute for low wages the most important element of the differential between gross and net wages. There is probably no single solution, and a satisfactory treatment of unemployment traps is probably the one which will bring together a combination of complementary activities, the effects of which have been as well measured out as possible.

Another major field of struggle against unemployment and exclusion is the enterprise. The continuous upkeep of employability in the framework of occupational activity promotes especially the extension of the active life of the oldest workers as, for example, in Denmark. *Employees and employers* are then jointly responsible actors in the maintenance of employability in a context of accelerated market changes and mutation of technologies and trades. What is involved is a win-win commitment, because the worker is ensured of remaining in activity, while the employer provides himself with the means of improving his or her performance by avoiding in particular problems connected with a shortage of labor. In this perspective, enterprises therefore put in place "policies for older workers" including provisions relating to the organization of work, the labor contract and close support measures for the older worker (training and adaptation to new activities).

The Thrusts of Developments in Employability

The step for the development of employability commenced by states relies on the mobilization of compensation funds, persons and institutions and on the creation of new employment opportunities.

Activation of funds consists, on the one hand, of devoting a more important share of expenditures allotted to dealing with unemployment to active measures and, on the other hand, of reducing accessibility to benefits (eligibility conditions, amounts and duration of compensation). Canada, whose program significantly bears the name *employment* insurance, has therefore set itself a double objective: support entry or return to employment and divert the unemployed from recourse to insurance by making access to benefits more difficult. In this country, for example, recipients of benefits may concurrently overlap these in full with earnings from work (within the limit of 25 percent of the amount of benefits) and see the amount of their allowances reduced when they have already enjoyed benefits during the five years preceding their application for benefits.

Activation of persons comes through individualized measures, preventive or curative, incentive or coercive, intended to strengthen the chances for a return to work and to improve the rate of activity.

Faced with a heavy increase in unemployment at the beginning of the 1990s, New Zealand noted that the previous solutions (subsidized job creation, measures aimed at restricting access to benefits) were no longer sufficient. The reforms then undertaken bore on the behavior of benefit recipients in the labor market. Various programs were set in place in order to oblige job-seekers and other categories of persons (disabled persons, single parents) to break with social assistance. Thus, for example, "community work programs" require unemployment benefit recipients to accept a job which has also benefits for communities, with recipients being allowed to receive, in addition to the benefits to which they are entitled, a non-taxable allowance and reimbursement of their actual expenses.

Activation of institutions involves the modernization of the public employment service and the mobilization of all institutional actors, and most particularly the state and the social partners. Employment services thus bring into operation tools which allow individual needs to be better targeted and long-term unemployment to be averted.

"Profiling" is, to this effect, a method and an instrument put in place in several countries, among which is the Netherlands, in order to sort out publics destined to benefit from differentiated treatment. The objective of this selection is to identify those persons most exposed to long-term unemployment, starting with professional criteria, staffs and factors connected with the labor market, in order to offer them individual support as quickly as possible.

In the United States, where profiling has been made general for all job-seekers receiving compensation, its use has been extended to other categories of "inactive" persons such as isolated young mothers and the poor, for whom an attempt is being made to drive them towards employment.

Activation of institutions also comes by broadening the benefits offered and improving their management. The National Employment Office of Slovakia, confronted with the difficulties of economies in transition, has, for example, put in place an aid program for the creation of enterprises, associating enterprises, regions, banks and private training centres, for job-seekers selected according to their motivation, qualifications and the credibility of their project.

The state and the social partners are attached moreover to creating conditions which further the development of opportunities offered in the labor market. The "job rotation" mechanism in Denmark constitutes an example of a practice intended to permit persons deprived of employment to (re)place their foot in the stirrup. Its principle resides in the possibility offered to employees to take leave (training, parental or sabbatical) during which they will receive an allowance, calculated as a percentage of the amount of the unemployment benefit, and will be replaced by a job-seeker.

Controlling Costs and Evaluating the Effectiveness of Employability Measures

In a context of massive and long-term unemployment, trends towards the activation of employment policies are in response to the will to better manage increasingly weighty budgets. The question is therefore one of discovering the best measures at the optimum cost benefit.

The choices made are of course not lacking in influence on the stability of systems: the cost will vary depending upon whether preference is given to curative or preventive measures, immediate access to employment or improvement of the qualification of individuals is favored, priority is given to assisting those persons most or least employable, local employability is being developed or a growth path is being built up with more stable but less numerous jobs. In their employment strategy, most countries continue to be confronted with these various dilemmas.

Evaluation of the effectiveness of the measures put in place, in economic terms, makes it obvious that mechanisms adapted to the local context and individualized are rather more effective than others. The fact remains that the economic gain acquired through active policies, in the absence of sufficiently developed indicators, is often not established.

Furthermore, it is always difficult to attribute the share of measures for the promotion of employability, and the share which is a product of the improved economic situation, in the improvement of unemployment rates. If all measures of the types acquiring occupational experience or development of human capital have a strong chance of reinforcing the employability of job-seekers, very little reliable information, nevertheless, exists concerning their effectiveness. It is clearly necessary to invest more in research and evaluation efforts in order to check the effectiveness of the various mechanisms.

The New Deal for Young People in the United Kingdom, for example, has been the object of a rigorous process of follow-up of its implementation and of evaluation starting with an identification of the various objectives of the program which are rather heterogeneous on the whole: participation of employers, reassignment of job-seekers, improvement of employability, reduction of costs, reduction of unemployment rates, etc.

Algeria, whose unemployment system was created recently (1994), has from the start integrated measures for the improvement of employability into its activity. Limited financial resources proportionately to its actual needs have nevertheless prompted it to proceed progressively by means of pilot projects. Even though in 50 percent of cases literacy constitutes a necessary prerequisite to any activity for the improvement of employability, the pilot project, including literacy courses and training in basic trades, will be broadened only after an analysis of the results and the agreement of the public authorities to commit additional financing.

Poland, which since 1998 has experienced an increase in the unemployment rate while resources committed to dealing with unemployment were decreasing, has also launched various measures intended to improve the efficacy of the expenditures committed. Satisfactory results, in terms of entry and reassignment, have been obtained, even though they concern only a small portion of the activities of employment offices, through "tripartite agreements" and entry programs for qualified young persons. Tripartite agreements enable employers themselves to choose candidates who will benefit from training adapted to the needs of the enterprise and who will be hired at the end of their training. As for the qualified young persons, who represent 45 percent of job-seekers, they can benefit, within the limit of the resources committed to these measures, from individualized entry plans composed of aids to seeking employment, training, try-outs with employers or subsidized jobs.

Flexibility, Employability, Security: An Inseparable Whole

Job flexibility and employability of employees are two performance factors of enterprises. Job flexibility and career breaks, determined by current labor market standards, impose upon workers a capacity for permanent adaptation to the evolution of social and economic needs.

However, an equilibrium must be ensured, so that job flexibility does not find expression in insecurity of employment and income for employees. Legislative or contractual safeguards have therefore been devised by certain states to accompany the easing of restrictions in manpower utilization with better protection of employees against its negative effects.

In the Netherlands, the *law on "flexcurity,"* implemented in 1999, attempts to reconcile flexibility and security. This law facilitates recourse to temporary employment in particular (fixed-term contracts and interim missions) while placing strict limits around recourse to this type of employment and endowing the employees concerned with specific rights (rights to training, transformation of the contract into a fixed-term contract after 36 months of successive contracts, interim contracts of indefinite duration, etc.).

Means for developing, preventively if possible, an aptitude for changing one's activity, trade or job are being put in place and trace the outlines of new systems bringing together all the actors concerned (workers—with or without employment, enterprises, social partners, state, associations, municipalities, etc.).

The adaptation of employees to changes presupposes in particular that employers ensure adequate visibility for their employees concerning the environment and objectives of the enterprise and the means of maintaining their employability in the labor market.

For their part, systems of protection against unemployment extend their activities beyond the payment of replacement income to workers without employment and propose various measures intended to facilitate entry or reassignment in the labor market. We are thus progressively witnessing the changeover from "unemployment insurance" to "employability insurance."

The prospect of methods for building and permanently maintaining employability from initial training, within the enterprise and during periods of interruption of occupational activity, until retirement is already evident in the existence of social rights, such as rights to training and leave, and in the development of transitional markets, such as employers' pools and subsidized contracts.

The promotion of employability comes down to permitting every individual throughout his/her life to organize the succession of his/her different activities while attempting to ensure the coherence of the whole system in order for employability to become the established instrument of occupational continuity.

Contributors

Mahrez Aït Belkacem, Director General, National Fund of Unemployment Insurance, Algeria.

Patrick Bollérot, Senior Research Officer, National Occupational Union for Employment in Industry and Commerce, France.

Isabelle Chabbert, Assistant, University Paris X, France.

Nancy Fedorovitch, Senior Policy Advisor, Department of Human Resources Development, Canada.

Ana Fotyga, Vice-president of the Supervisory Council of the Social Insurance Institution, Poland.

Bernard Gazier, Professor, Centre le Titien, University Paris I, France.

Nicole Kerschen, Senior Researcher, National Centre for Social Research, France.

Tony Kieran, Consultant, Ireland.

Ross McKay, Special Advisor, Social Policy Agency, Department of Social Welfare, New Zealand.

Nigel Meager, Associate Director, Institute for Employment Studies (IES), University of Sussex, Brighton, United Kingdom.

Marjolein Peters, Consultant, Small Business Research and Consultancy, EIM International, Netherlands.

Helmut Rudolph, Senior Research Officer, Institute for Employment Research, Federal Employment Office, Germany.

Javoslav Sumný, Director General, National Labour Office, Slovak Republic.

Koen Van Den Heuvel, Consultant, National Bank of Belgium, Belgium.

Wim Zwinkels, Consultant, Small Business Research and Consultancy, EIM International, Netherlands.

Index